CW01430131

WALKING IN CATALUNYA - GIRONA PYRENEES

35 HIKES IN GARROTXA, CADÍ-MOIXERÓ NATURAL PARK AND RIPOLLÈS

by Nike Werstroh and Jacint Mig

CICERONE

JUNIPER HOUSE, MURLEY MOSS,
OXENHOLME ROAD, KENDAL, CUMBRIA LA9 7RL
www.cicerone.co.uk

© Nike Werstroh and Jacint Mig 2023
First edition 2023
ISBN: 978 1 78631 163 4

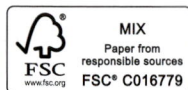

Printed in India by Replika Press Pvt Ltd using responsibly sourced paper.
A catalogue record for this book is available from the British Library.
All photographs are by the authors unless otherwise stated.

lovelljohns.com

Route mapping by Lovell Johns www.lovelljohns.com
Contains OpenStreetMap.org data © OpenStreetMap con-
tributors, CC-BY-SA. NASA relief data courtesy of ESRI.

Updates to this guide

While every effort is made by our authors to ensure the accuracy of guide-
books as they go to print, changes can occur during the lifetime of an edition. Any updates that we know of for this guide will be on the Cicerone
website (www.cicerone.co.uk/1163/updates), so please check before planning your trip. We also advise that you check information about such things
as transport, accommodation and shops locally. Even rights of way can be
altered over time. We are always grateful for information about any discrep-
ancies between a guidebook and the facts on the ground, sent by email
to updates@cicerone.co.uk or by post to Cicerone, Juniper House, Murley
Moss, Oxenholme Road, Kendal, LA9 7RL.

Register your book: To sign up to receive free updates, special offers
and GPX files where available, register your book in your Cicerone library
at www.cicerone.co.uk.

*Front cover: Pedraforca views from the demanding steep trail to Comabona
(Walk 34)*

CONTENTS

Walking away from La Tosa (Walk 28)

Acknowledgements

We would like to thank the Catalan Tourist Board for their help and enthusiastic support during the research. Thank you to Aicard Guinovart i Marquès and the London office, and to everyone who helped with our research from the local tourist boards of Bagà, Ripollès, Berguedà and Alt Empordà.

Also a special thank you to Adriana Ramon from Itinerànnia for suggesting some amazing trails and areas to explore. Thank you for all the knowledge and tips that you shared with us during the research.

Thank you to Joe Williams and everyone from the Cicerone team who believed in this project and worked on this book.

Note on mapping

The route maps in this guide are derived from publicly available data, databases and crowd-sourced data. As such they have not been through the detailed checking procedures that would generally be applied to a published map from an official mapping agency. However, we have reviewed them closely in light of local knowledge as part of the preparation of this guide.

Mountain safety

Every mountain walk has its dangers, and those described in this guidebook are no exception. All who walk or climb in the mountains should recognise this and take responsibility for themselves and their companions along the way. The author and publisher have made every effort to ensure that the information contained in this guide was correct when it went to press, but, except for any liability that cannot be excluded by law, they cannot accept responsibility for any loss, injury or inconvenience sustained by any person using this book.

International distress signal *(emergency only)*
Six blasts on a whistle (and flashes with a torch after dark) spaced evenly for one minute, followed by a minute's pause. Repeat until an answer is received. The response is three signals per minute followed by a minute's pause.

Helicopter rescue
The following signals are used to communicate with a helicopter:

Help needed: raise both arms above head to form a 'Y'

Help not needed: raise one arm above head, extend other arm downward

Emergency telephone numbers
112 or 062 for the Guardia Civil
(Civil Guard - for mountain rescue services and other accidents)

Weather reports
www.meteo.cat or www.meteoblue.com

Mountain rescue can be very expensive – be adequately insured.

Symbols used on route maps

route	▲ peak	✳ viewpoint
alternative route	✕ pass	• other feature
Ⓢ start point	■ building	• water feature
Ⓕ finish point	◖ cave	refreshment
ⓈⒻ start/finish point	≍ bridge	castle
Ⓕ alternative finish point	= footbridge	🅿 parking
➤ route direction	🏛 picnic area	ⓘ tourist information
woodland	⛪ monastery	
urban areas	† shrine/cross	
station/railway	church/chapel/hermitage	
cable car		
⇧ unmanned hut/refuge		
⬆ manned hut/refuge		
⛺ campsite		

Relief
in metres

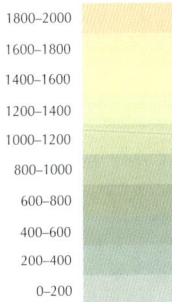

1800–2000	
1600–1800	
1400–1600	
1200–1400	
1000–1200	
800–1000	
600–800	
400–600	
200–400	
0–200	

SCALE: 1:50,000

0 kilometres 0.5   1
0 miles   0.5

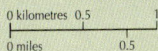

Contour lines are drawn at 25m intervals and highlighted at 100m intervals.

SCALE: 1:25,000

0 kilometres 0.25   0.5
0 miles   0.25

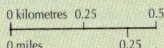

1:25,000 maps are used in the following walks: 2, 3, 10, 13, 15, 20 and 24

GPX files for all routes can be downloaded free at www.cicerone.co.uk/1163/GPX.

ROUTE SUMMARY TABLE

Walk	Name	Start/Finish	Route
1	Puig de Bassegoda	Collet de la Teia	circular
2	Muga Gorge	Bassegoda Park	there and back
3	Beuda to El Mont	Beuda	circular
4	Sadernes to Salt de Brull	Sadernes	there and back
5	Volcà de Santa Margarida and Croscat	Can Blanc	circular
6	Puig Rodó and Sant Miquel del Corb	Les Preses	circular
7	Salt de la Coromina and Camí Ral	Els Hostalets d'en Bas	circular
8	Puigsacalm from Joanates	Joanates	circular
9	Puigsacalm from Coll de Bracons	Coll de Bracons	there and back
10	Salt de Sallent	Sant Privat d'en Bas	circular
11	Oix to Santa Maria d'Escales	Oix	circular
12	Castell de Besora	Montesquiu	circular
13	Gorg de Masica	Vallfogona de Ripollès	there and back
14	Via Romana	Sant Pau de Segúries	there and back
15	Camprodon to Sant Antoni	Camprodon	circular
16	Serra Cavallera ridge from Camprodon	Camprodon	circular
17	Camí de Carboneres	Setcases	circular
18	Gra de Fajol	Vall de Ter	circular
19	Pic de la Dona and Bastiments	Vallter 2000	circular
20	Seven gorges trail	Campdevànol	circular
21	Taga from Ribes de Freser	Ribes de Freser	there and back
22	Queralbs to Font de l'Home Mort	Queralbs	circular
23	Camí Vell de Núria	Queralbs/Núria	linear
24	Puigmal	Núria	there and back
25	Pic de Finestrelles	Núria	circular
26	Salt del Grill and Coma de Vaca	Queralbs	circular
27	Falgars and Roc de la Lluna	La Pobla de Lillet	circular
28	La Tosa	Trencapinyes car park	circular
29	Penyes Altes de Moixeró	Gréixer	circular
30	Els Empedrats	Els Empedrats car park	circular
31	Via del Nicolau	Guardiola de Berguedà	there and back
32	Pedraforca Superior	Mirador de Gresolet	circular
33	Saldes to Gresolet	Saldes	circular
34	Comabona	Santuari de Gresolet	circular
35	Pedraforca 360	Gósol	circular

Distance	Time	Gain/Loss	Grade	Page
13.5km	5hr 30min–6hr	920m	3	25
10.5km	3hr 30min	260m	1	28
11km	4hr 20min	850m	2	31
17.5km	5hr 30min–6hr	780m	3	35
12km	3hr 30min	350m	1	39
13km	5hr	850m	2	42
11km	3hr 30min	550m	2	45
11km	6hr–6hr 30min	1120m	3+	49
9km	3hr	420m	2	53
12km	4hr 30min	700m	2	55
12.5km	4hr	450m	2	59
10km	3hr	490m	2	63
11km	4hr–4hr 30min	500m	1	67
11km	4hr	600m	1	73
5km	2hr	420m	1	75
18.5km	6hr 30min–7hr	1030m	3	78
11.5km	4hr 30min	750m	2	82
12.5km	5hr 30min–6hr	1110m	3	86
12km	4hr 30min–5hr	900m	3	90
9km	2hr 30min–3hr	250m	1	94
13km	5hr	1170m	3	97
14.5km	5hr–5hr 30min	940m	2	100
8km	3hr	1050m/265m	2	103
9km	4hr	950m	3	107
12km	5hr	910m	3	110
19km	8hr	1530m	3	113
18km	5hr 30min	1030m	2	117
16km	6hr	1300m	3	125
17km	6hr 30min	1350m	3	128
11.5km	4hr 30min	820m	2	131
12.5km	3hr 30min	430m	1	134
8.5km	5hr 30min	1160m	3+	137
13km	4hr–4hr 30min	680m	2	140
13.5km	5hr 30min	1300m	3	144
17.5km	5hr 30min	820m	2	147

The final stretch to the top of Bastiments is quite challenging (Walk 19)

INTRODUCTION

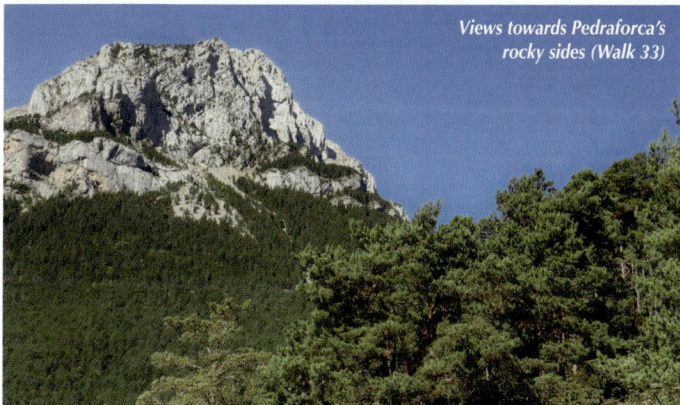

Views towards Pedraforca's rocky sides (Walk 33)

Leave behind Girona's medieval walls, narrow cobbled streets with cosy restaurants and riverside lined with colourful houses and you will find a network of trails twisting among the volcanic cones and meandering through rocky gorges with spectacular waterfalls in the Garrotxa. Or you can follow narrow paths that climb to long-forgotten ruins and hidden churches on the lush mountains of the Alta Garrotxa.

Dotted with charming villages, medieval stone bridges, fresh mountain rivers and rugged mountain peaks with far-reaching views, the diverse landscape of the Girona province provides endless trails to explore.

In the north, the majestic Pyrenees mountain range forms a natural border between Spain and France. Blanketed in snow in the winter, the many great ski slopes – attracting winter sport lovers – come to life.

The peaks may be snow-capped well into the spring, but when most of the white blanket melts away, fresh mountain streams race down the slopes, wildflowers carpet the meadows and hikers replace the skiers. Paths cross the boundless alpine meadows, noisy with cattle bells and the sound of the marmots. Trails climb with far-reaching, dizzying views and a breathtaking panorama greets hikers on any of the peaks on clear summer days.

Built at spectacular locations, manned and unmanned mountain huts give shelter to hikers who follow one of the several long-distance trails traversing the Pyrenees. However, there are countless delightful day walks to choose from if you want to explore the Girona Pyrenees.

The mountains of the Pre-Pyrenees may have a lower altitude, but they are just as spectacular as the high Pyrenees and offer a more varied landscape and snow-free walking trails earlier in the year. The iconic double peak of Pedraforca is thought to be one of the most photographed mountains in Catalunya. Painted with pink in the early morning and orange in the evening, blanketed with snow in the winter and wrapped in dancing clouds on summer afternoons, no two pictures of this fascinating mountain are the same.

Although proud of its own language and identity, Catalunya has been part of Spain since the 15th century, when King Ferdinand of Aragon married Queen Isabella of Castile. The region initially kept its institutions, but it was then integrated into the Spanish state until the 19th century, when a renewed sense of identity lead to the campaign for political autonomy. In 1931, when Spain became a republic, Catalunya was given broad autonomy. However, during Franco's rule (1939–1975) this autonomy was revoked, and Catalan nationalism was repressed. After Franco's death, Spain's restoration of democracy started, and in 1979 Catalunya was given a statute of autonomy and recognised nationality. The Catalan language became a joint official language. Recent years have seen some struggles for independence, and the political situation can, at times, be complicated.

Catalunya is vast, and in this book we only explore parts of the Girona province, mainly the areas and mountain ranges of the Girona

Pyrenees and Pre-Pyrenees, including the regions of Garrotxa, Ripollès and the Cadí-Moixeró Natural Park. Most of the trails can be enjoyed between April and October; however, the lower areas in the Garrotxa can even be attempted in the winter months, and they are easily accessible from Barcelona, Girona, Olot, Ripoll and Berga.

Hiking and biking trails are well promoted, and active holidays are encouraged for the growing number of people who want to explore Catalunya beyond the Costa Brava. Some routes and areas see a great number of hikers, and recently there has been a great effort to guide visitors towards the more rural areas in Catalunya. However, you can certainly find quiet, lesser-used trails in each area covered in this book.

Catalunya can provide hikers with endless trails, from easy strolls to more demanding walks. The friendly locals welcome the growing number of people who want to explore the fascinating and diverse areas on foot.

GEOGRAPHY AND GEOLOGY

Catalunya lies on the Iberian Peninsula, south of the Pyrenees mountain range. Its eastern shores are washed by the Mediterranean sea, and its climate is shaped by the sea and the mountains. Catalunya consists of four provinces: Barcelona, Girona, Lleida and Tarragona. This book focuses on the Girona province.

The varied landscape includes the volcanic Garrotxa, the Alta Garrotxa and the Cadí-Moixeró range. These regions form part of the Pre-Pyrenees and the southern slopes of the Pyrenees, with deep gorges, waterfalls, and alpine meadows.

The Garrotxa is a monogenetic volcanic field shaped by some 40 volcanoes, each representing a single period of eruption. The area became active some 700,000 years ago and the most recent activity was just over 10,000 years ago.

The Serra de Cadí range was formed between 66 million and 2.5 million years ago as a results of the orogenesis of the Pyrenees, and it is characterised by alpine folding. The northern slopes are made of Jurassic materials and the peaks are Eocene limestone.

The Serra de Moixeró is older than the Serra de Cadí, and it formed during the late Paleozoic continental collision. Devonian limestone is found on the peaks, while schist is more common at lower elevations and in the east.

One of the highest mountain ranges in Europe, the Pyrenees were formed by the collision between the European plate and the Iberian microplate during the Paleogene period (55 to 25 million years ago). After the uplift, intense erosion and isostatic readjustments shaped the chain. The eastern part of the Pyrenees consists of granite and gneissose rocks.

Clockwise from top-left: Alpine Sea Holly (Eryngium alpinum); the Blue monkshood (Aconitum napellus) is the most poisonous plant in the Pyrenees; mushroom picking has a long tradition in Catalunya; Liverleaf (Hepatica nobilis)

PLANTS AND FLOWERS

The vegetation in the Garrotxa is mainly Mediterranean. Oak and beech are the dominant tree species and there are over 1100 identified plant species in the Natural Park of Garrotxa Volcanic Zone.

Red pine, fir and beech can be found on the lower slopes of the Pre-Pyrenees in the Cadí-Moixeró Natural Park. Above 1800m black pine is the most common species and alpine meadows usually replace trees above 2000m.

In the summer spectacular alpine flowers bloom on the slopes of the Girona Pyrenees. From late May you can spot delicate orchids, such as the bee orchid and the early spider orchid, among many others. You may also find several varieties of gentians flowering throughout the season. The limestone provides a perfect home to many alpine plants, such as species of the saxifrage and thistles, and – on the meadows – you can admire different species of lilies.

The Pyrenean Mountain pines can push the treeline up to 2600m in the Pyrenees. Black pines can be found up to 2100m, and on lower slopes Scots pine, beech and birch are the most common species. Below 1000m the hillsides are usually populated by sweet chestnut, hornbeam and oaks.

WILDLIFE

Much of Catalunya (except the mountainous areas) enjoys a Mediterranean climate, therefore the animals that are found in Mediterranean climates elsewhere – for example, wild boars, red foxes, roe deer and red squirrels – can also be found in Catalunya. If you hike in the Girona Pyrenees in the late spring or summer, you can almost certainly spot two iconic mammals: the shy Pyrenean chamois skilfully navigating on the steep slopes and the alpine marmots. The marmots were reintroduced to the Pyrenees in 1948, and they prefer the higher slopes between 1000m and 3200m. You can mostly see them on the trails near Vall de Núria and Vallter 2000. Even if you don't see them, you might hear the whistling noise they make to communicate with each other. They spend the summer months eating to build up fat for the winter when they hibernate in their burrows for about seven months.

After the bear numbers fell to only a handful of individuals in the 1990s, three brown bears (from Slovenia) were reintroduced to the Pyrenees. It is estimated that there are about 70 brown bears living in mainly the central part of the Pyrenees. Their numbers are slowly growing.

There are a small number of grey wolves in the Pyrenees. Some live on the eastern part of the mountain range.

You can spot birds of prey, such as the griffon vulture, which has an impressive two and a half-metre wingspan.

15

Always give cows with calves a very wide berth

Snakes are usually wary of humans and many of them are harmless; however, there are some venomous snakes – such as the *Vipera seoanei*, or the asp viper – in the mountainous areas of northern Catalunya.

Cows – although not a wild animal – are often seen on the meadows where they graze during the warmer months. Never walk between calf and mother, and always give them a wide berth – at least 30 metres – and even divert from the path if it is necessary and the terrain allows.

GETTING THERE

The best way to get to Catalunya is to fly to Barcelona or Girona and then take the local buses or trains or hire a car to get around.

Barcelona is well connected with other European cities and numerous airlines (including the well-known budget airlines) offer flights from various airports. There are also plenty of direct flights to Barcelona and a few to Girona from various UK airports. As always, shop around for the best deals.

If you choose to drive from the UK, make sure you have all the right paperwork and insurance for your car and the driver. Take one of the many ferries between Dover and Calais or, for a faster journey, take the Eurotunnel. To shorten the drive in France, choose Brittany Ferries overnight sails from Portsmouth to La Havre or Caen. There is also an option to sail straight to Santander or Bilbao in Northern Spain.

The main station in Barcelona (Estació de Sants) serves suburban and national, as well as international, routes. The following websites can help you to plan international routes from European cities:

www.raileurope.com
www.thetrainline.com
www.renfe.com

GETTING AROUND

Buses
There is a bus service from Barcelona, Girona, Olot, Ripoll and Berga to other towns and villages, but buses in rural areas are not frequent and you are strongly advised to check the timetable locally before setting off. If you are planning to get to and from the walks described in this book by buses only, it is highly advisable to seek information at the local tourist office. It is probably better to spend a few days in the same area. There may be some on-demand bus services in the Garrotxa. See Appendix A.

Trains
From Barcelona, there are train services to many of the major towns that are located close to the trails, such as Girona, Ripoll and Ribes de Freser. However, in most cases you will have to combine the train and bus journeys and plan your day carefully.

www.renfe.com

Walk 23 (Camí Vell de Núria) is a linear trail. However, from Núria

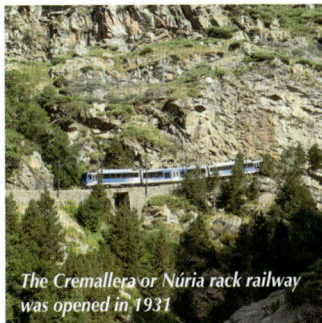
The Cremallera or Núria rack railway was opened in 1931

you can descend back to Queralbs by the rack railway (it is advisable to pre-book your tickets).

www.valldenuria.cat/en

Car
Driving around with a hire car is an easy way to explore this part of Catalunya. Many places and trails are easily accessible by car, and there are usually places to park at the beginning of the trails.

Most of the linear walks in this book are not too long, and because of the lack of transport they are always described as a there-and-back trail (Walk 2, Walk 9, Walk 13, Walk 14, Walk 21, Walk 24 and Walk 31). When you are planning your day always make sure that you allow enough time for each trail.

The most convenient option is probably to hire a car at Barcelona or Girona airport on your arrival. You can also find car hire companies in bigger towns, but as always you can get better deals by booking in advance online.

Taxis

If you want to book a taxi, you can seek information about local companies from the local tourist offices.

BASES

Olot, which has several hotels, restaurants, cafés and shops, is a good base to explore the trails in the Garrotxa. There are also guest houses in the Bas Valley and in the villages near Olot, and there are many campsites to choose from in the area. There is a campsite with bungalows and an astronomical observatory near Albanyà.

Bagà and Guardiola de Berguadà, which have shops and restaurants, could be good bases to explore the trails in the Cadí-Moixeró Natural Park. You can also find accommodation in picturesque Saldes or Gósol at the foot of Pedraforca. There are also plenty of good campsites in the area where you can spend a few days.

Ripoll can be a good place to start to explore the Ripollès. The town has accommodation, restaurants and shops, and there is also a train service to Ribes de Freser. The lively Ribes de Freser is a perfect base to take a day trip to Núria. There is a hotel and also a campsite in Núria if you want to spend a few days exploring the mountains in this magical place.

Setcases and Camprodon cater to tourists with hotels, guest houses, campsites and restaurants throughout the year.

ACCOMMODATION

Choice of accommodation is always a personal one, taking into account your budget and preferences. There are plenty of hotels and self-catering options to choose from, especially in the towns, and there are a range of options available in more touristic villages.

You might opt to tackle several day trips in the same area, or – depending on the length of your holiday – you might consider splitting your time between different bases. If you decide to stay in one base, you can still enjoy different areas, as many places are easily reached in a day trip. Make sure you book through a trusted website. When you are looking for accommodation, you might want to look at the campsites as well, even if you are not planning to sleep in a tent or caravan, as there are several campsites that offer self-catering bungalows. There is a list of campsites in Appendix B.

There is an increased interest in rural tourism in Catalunya, and you can check the official guide to tourism establishments in Catalunya on this website: http://establimentsturistics.gencat.cat.

WHEN TO GO AND WHAT TO TAKE

You will almost certainly be able to find a suitable walk between spring and autumn in this book. Even in April, snow is common on higher ground, but you can find some lovely walks in the Garrotxa in the spring, and maybe even in the winter. Save the trails in the Pyrenees for the summer months. The summer months are generally hot in Catalunya, but in the mountains the temperatures are a lot cooler and perfect for walking.

There might be more rainy days in the spring and autumn, and storms are also common in the summer, especially in the mountains. The Garrotxa, particularly around Olot, is considered the wettest part of Catalunya.

Pack what you would normally take for a day walk, and always carry

The steep, stony descent from the summit of Puigmal (Walk 24)

a waterproof jacket and a warm fleece or jumper in the mountains, as it can be cool and windy on the summits, and thunderstorms can develop quickly, bringing low visibility, cold temperatures and hailstorms, even on warm summer days.

Comfortable hiking boots, sun cream and a sun hat are essential, and always carry ample water, especially in the summer months. Make sure you take your camera to capture the amazing landscape.

Many of the routes in this guide can be successfully navigated without a map, but it is always advisable to have a map on hand (paper or digital). Look out for the Alpina maps in the local bookshops or online at www.editorialalpina.com. Also check out the handy interactive maps with route planning tools on www.itinerannia.net/en.

In case of emergency, call 112. If you see a rescue helicopter and you don't need help, raise one arm above your head and extend the other arm downwards to indicate an 'N' for no. If you or someone else nearby needs help, raise both arms above your head to indicate 'Y' for yes.

LANGUAGE

Most local people are bilingual and speak Catalan as well as Spanish. Most of the signs are in Catalan and also in Spanish, especially in areas popular with tourists. At restaurants the menus are in Catalan as well as in Spanish. If you speak or understand some basic Spanish, you will have no problems in the rural areas. English is, however, widely spoken, especially among the younger people. Appendix C has a glossary of some Catalan and Spanish words that you might find useful.

WAYMARKING

The GR (Gran Recorrido/Gran Recorregut) long-distance trails are marked with white above red stripes and their numbers appear on the signpost – for example, GR11 (Walk 23).

The PR-C (Pequeno Recorrido/ Petit Recorregut) trails are usually less than 20km long, and they are marked with yellow and white and a number, such as PR-C 125 (Walk 30).

Itinerànnia has an extensive network of waymarked trails that crisscross the Garrotxa, Ripollès and Alt Empordà areas. A frequent horizontal yellow sign on trees and rocks is used to mark the trails.

At most junctions there is a signpost with the place name (for example, in Walk 1, Coll de Bassegoda, AE078) and in the route description the place name and the number of the junction is mentioned for your reference.

The signposts at junctions usually have several arrows indicating the direction and distances to various towns and villages. An arrow with a red tip marks the direction and the shortest distance to the named village or town. Alternative routes are described on the signpost – for example, Puigsacalm pel Puig dels Llops (Walk 8). However, you can also see arrows with a green tip; these are used to mark circular routes, usually around a town or village.

There are some information boards with a map of the area located in towns and villages where you start a trail.

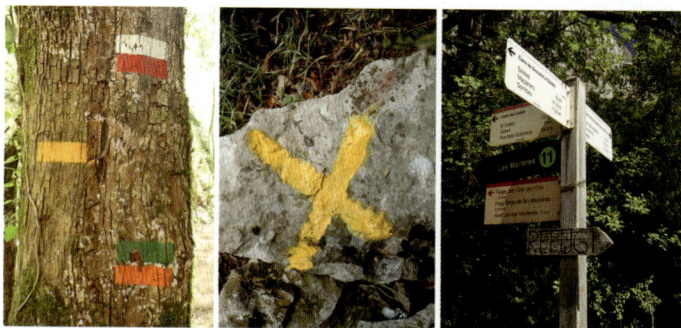

Common waymarkers; Itinerannia network wrong way marker; waymarkers in the Cadí-Moixeró Natural Park

The trails in this book make use of the Itinerànnia's waymarked paths in the area, as well as some sections of the long-distance trails and PR-C routes, or sometimes a combination of these. The description always mentions what signs you should look out for. Occasionally there are some signs painted on rocks in the Girona Pyrenees, and it is always pointed out in the description if you have to look out for these. The marked trails usually use an 'X' (in trail colours) to mark the wrong path at junctions.

USING THIS GUIDE

The walks in this guide are divided into three sections. Each section begins with a brief introduction to the area and gives some information about potential bases from which to plan your walks.

An information box at the start of each walk provides the follow-ing information: the start/finish point (including GPS coordinates), the length of the walk in kilometres, the total ascent/descent in metres, a dif-ficulty rating (see the grading infor-mation below), the length of time the walk is likely to take, details about refreshments and access informa-tion that might be useful to plan your day.

Springs for drinking water in the mountains are mentioned, but don't rely on them entirely and make sure you always carry ample water for the day.

Places and features that appear on the accompanying maps are shown in **bold** in the route descriptions.

The times and distances given in the route information boxes and route summary table are from start to finish. Some trails – because of their remote-ness and/or lack of transport – are described as there-and-back routes, and the times and distances are given accordingly. If you are planning to use buses, always check the bus timetable locally, or arrange a taxi in advance if necessary.

The relative difficulty of each walk (compared with the other walks in this book) is classified by grade. The grading in this guide is only an indica-tor; bad weather can make any walk more challenging. Clouds can arrive quickly in the mountains and can leave you with very limited visibility. The grading is:

• **Grade 1**: easy and/or short walk; trail is without any significant ascent/descent
• **Grade 2**: moderate, medium-length or longer walk, but mostly on easy or moderate terrain
• **Grade 3**: a longer walk and/or more difficult terrain
• **Grade 3+**: difficult terrain with easy scrambling or aided sections where you have to use your hands (Walk 8, Walk 32)

The times provided – both for the walks themselves and between land-marks – are approximate. The times given are fairly generous but do not take into account longer breaks for picnics or visiting attractions. Once you have tried some walks using this guide, you will be able to see how your own pace compares to the times given and you can adjust your planning accordingly.

Access to the trails is described in as much detail as possible. To help identify the exact location, GPS coordinates for the trail starting points are also given. Where public transport is available, this is indicated in the information box for the walk.

Where a waymarked trail is used, the trail number and the colours of the waymarking/signage are mentioned. Occasionally, the trail described takes an unmarked path or a path marked with cairns, but this is always pointed out in the description.

Each route is illustrated with either 1:50,000 or 1:25,000 mapping. Features highlighted in bold in the step-by-step route description should be those that appear on these map extracts.

The book's aim is to introduce some amazing trails in the Girona province. There are plenty of other trails of different lengths and difficulty levels in each area which aren't in this book.

Appendices

Appendix A offers some useful contacts, and Appendix B lists campsites in the region and provides web links to further accommodation options. A Catalan–Spanish–English glossary can be found in Appendix C.

GPX tracks

GPX tracks for the routes in this guidebook are available to download free at www.cicerone.co.uk/1163/GPX. If you have not bought the book through the Cicerone website, or if you've bought the book without opening an account, please register your purchase in your Cicerone library to access GPX and update information.

A GPS device is an excellent aid to navigation, but you should also carry a map and a compass and know how to use them. GPX files are provided in good faith, but in view of the profusion of formats and devices, neither the author nor the publisher accepts responsibility for their use. We provide files in a single standard GPX format that works on most devices and systems, but you may need to convert files to your preferred format using a GPX converter, such as www.gpsvisualizer.com or one of the many other apps and online converters available.

GARROTXA

Before reaching Salt de Brull, a short section of Walk 4 goes into the river bed

Views to the volcanic Garrotxa (Walk 3)

The varied landscape of Garrotxa is made up of the Garrotxa Volcanic Zone – shaped by some 40 volcanoes – and the mountains of the Alta Garrotxa. The forested volcanic cones are separated with fertile land dotted with charming traditional villages. To enjoy the extensive views of the diverse landscape of the Garrotxa, climb Puigsacalm (Walk 8 and 9).

Follow one of the rocky gorges with rushing water that cut through the mountains of the Alta Garrotxa, where trails meander to hidden churches (Walk 11) or waterfalls (Walk 4). From the peaks you can enjoy views towards the nearby mountains in the Pyrenees (Walk 1).

If you need a break from hiking, why not wander the cobbled streets of Besalú, one of the best-preserved medieval towns in Catalunya, or sample some local food in one of the many restaurants? Olot is well connected to Girona and it is a good base to explore the area from, with shops, restaurants and accommodation. You can find somewhere to stay in one of the villages closer to the trails, and there are also many great campsites with bungalows in the area.

If you want to spend the evenings stargazing and are interested in astronomy, the International Dark-Sky Association-certified Observatori Astronòmic Albanyà, located near Bassegoda Park campsite (www.bassegodapark.com), offers regular educational tours.

WALK 1
Puig de Bassegoda

Start/finish	Collet de la Teia, N42.316516, E2.680327
Distance	13.5km
Total ascent/descent	920m
Grade	3
Time	5hr 30min–6hr
Refreshments	None along the way.
Access	From Albanyà (located at the end of GI-511 road) head towards Bassegoda Park and then follow the narrow road to a fork in the road about 1.5km from Bassegoda Park. Go left and follow the narrow winding road uphill for another 4.5km to Collet de la Teia. There are spaces to park.

This full-day walk takes you through lush forests and rocky mountainsides with remarkable views to the Pyrenees and across the Alta Garrotxa. The trail described is waymarked, and there are also some helpful rustic wooden signs in the forest.

Follow the sealed road on the mountainside towards Sant Miquel de Bassegoda for about 1km and then take the track on the left by the Sant Martí de Corsavell sign. Follow the track for about 800 metres and arrive at the 12th–13th-century **Sant Martí de Corsavell Church**. From the building continue on the path marked with yellow signs. You might also notice some red markers, but follow the yellow signs. Climb on a stony path through forest and about 15–20min from the church reach a sealed road and go left. Shortly after at Collada de Can Nou, AE73 junction, go right towards San Miquel de Bassagoda and the refuge.

The sealed road becomes track as you ascend, pass a font and a few minutes later reach an old farmhouse, **Can Nou**. (There, you find some information about the refuge.) After the building at Bassegoda-Can Nou, AE75 junction, keep right on the path alongside the fence. Follow the yellow signs uphill through forest for about 10min and arrive at **Refugi de Bassegoda** (Can Galan). Enjoy some amazing views and then continue uphill through forest towards Puig de Bassegoda. Mountains fill the horizon as far as you can see and occasionally the towering Puig de Bassegoda comes into view as you ascend the stony path. Reach a dirt

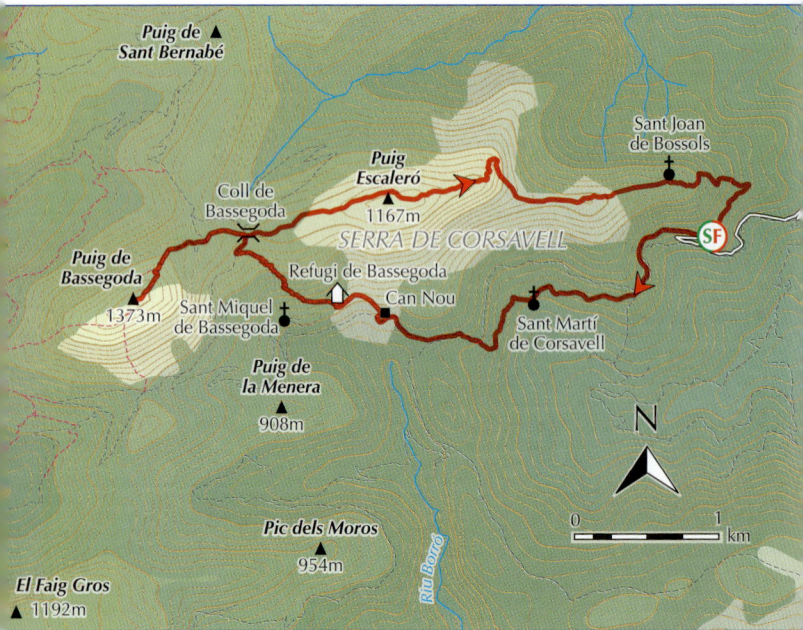

track at Sota Coll de Bassegoda, AE077 junction, and go right. A few minutes later at **Coll de Bassegoda**, AE078, take the path on the left marked with a wooden sign, Pico de Bassegoda (you will return to this junction from the peak).

Following the yellow signs reach and cross a track, and the path continues on its other side. Shortly after, reach another track and go right. At a clearing you can enjoy the first views towards the mountains of the Pyrenees. Alongside the yellow signs you can also spot orange and green signs as you climb steeply towards the rocky peak. Look out for the signs and turn right to scramble up on the rocks. There is also a very short aided section just below the summit. From **Puig de Bassegoda** (alt. 1373m) you can enjoy the 360-degree panorama. To the north the scenery is dominated by the mountains of the Pyrenees.

From the peak retrace your steps to **Coll de Bassegoda**, AE078 junction (about 30min from the peak). Take care on the rocks and then on the steep downhill sections, as it can be muddy and slippery. From the col continue straight on towards Albanyà pel Pin Muga. Follow the yellow signs through the forest, which is scattered with rocks, with an occasional glimpse towards the mountains of the

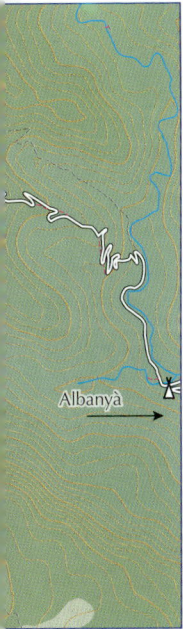

Can Nou is an 18th-century farmhouse which is passed just before reaching the Refugi de Bassegoda

Albanyà

Pyrenees on your left. Soon the descent starts. Walk across a rocky area and then descend through forest. After a short climb walk through rocky terrain again. The church of Sant Joan de Bossols at the far end of the ridge comes into view about 50min from Coll de Bessagoda. Zigzag steeply downhill and soon you can spot the buildings of Can Nou down below.

After a steep descent walk alongside a rock wall with some views towards the church on the ridge. The path splits; keep left towards the church (the path on the right heads back to the refuge). Follow the narrow ridge and ignore another path marked with yellow on the left. Descend and then walk through forest. Reach the ruins of the Romanesque-style **Sant Joan de Bossols Church** about an hour after you caught the first glimpse of it. According to documents it was constructed before 1413 and was abandoned around 1910. You can skirt around the ruins for further views.

From the ruins follow the yellow signs downhill through forest. Zigzag downhill for about 10–15min and reach a track at Serra de Bossols, AG9, and go right. About 400 metres later arrive back at the starting point.

WALK 2
Muga Gorge

Start/finish	Bassegoda Park (Campsite), N42.306951, E2.708909
Distance	10.5km (there and back)
Total ascent/descent	260m
Grade	1
Time	3hr 30min
Refreshments	None along the way.
Access	From Albanyà take Carretera d'Albanyà a Bassegoda to Bassegoda Park; the campsite is a great place to stay for a few days while exploring the area.
Public transport	Bus from Figueres to Albanyà, and Bassegoda Park is a 15-minute walk from the village.

This easy there-and-back route follows a scenic rocky gorge to a 19th-century stone bridge and then continues to the ruins of Castell del Serrat of Albanyà. Don't miss the short detour that leads to a curious circular building, a medieval pigeon house, just before the castle.

From the entrance of Bassegoda Park campsite follow the sealed road alongside the gorge, passing some numbered parking places, for about 1.5km. Leave this sealed road (in a forked **junction**) to the right on a track by the gorge towards Sant Bartomeu de Picaro.

Notice a building on the other side of the gorge and shortly after take the path on the right and **ford** the river (you might have to take your boots off). Keep left near the gate and follow the narrow path with the river on your left. At the signpost go right towards

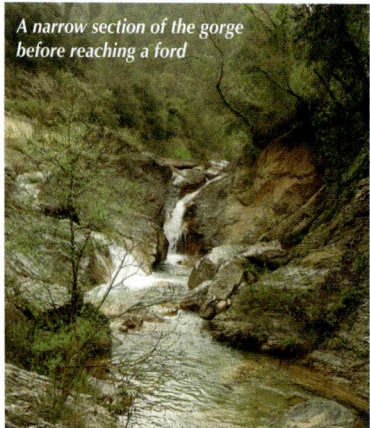
A narrow section of the gorge before reaching a ford

Casal-Castell del Serrat i Colomar. The path goes slightly up and away from the river.

After about 3km, when the path splits, keep right (the other path drops down to the river bank) and reach a track. Go left towards Casal-Castell by the signpost.

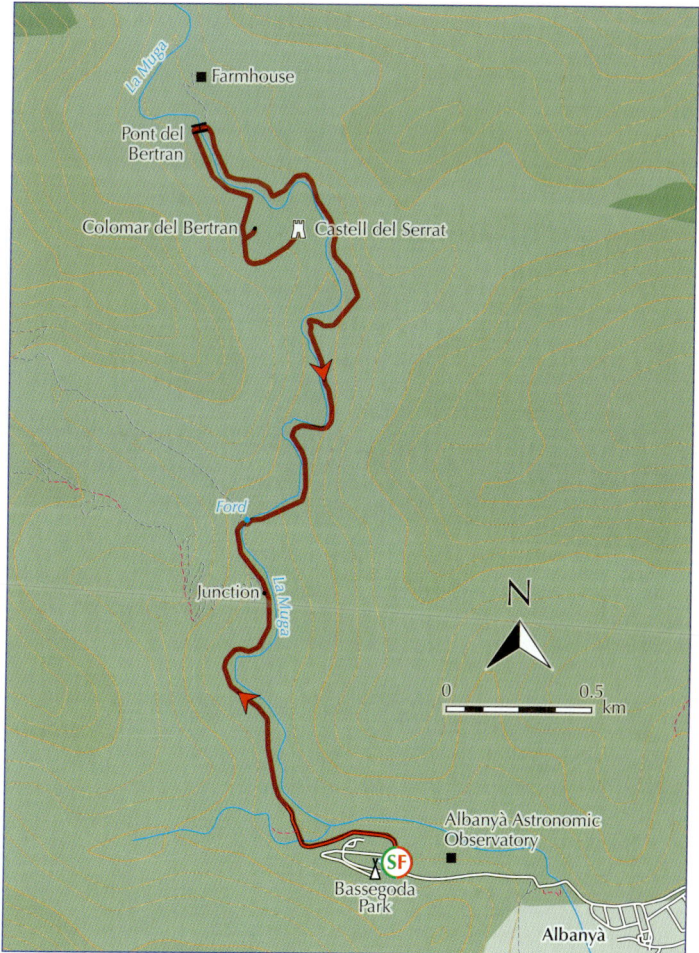

Shortly after, the dirt track becomes a sealed road and you can spot the ruins of the castle on the other side of the river.

Notice some steps on the left heading down to a picturesque spot by the river; however, continue on the track. Notice a fording place – it is not ideal to cross the river there so continue on the track. Shortly after a farm house on the hillside comes into view leave the dirt track to the left and cross the bridge, **Pont del Bertran** (Pont de Molí d'en Bertran), constructed in 1891. After the bridge keep left on the narrow path that joins a track. As you follow this track look out for the Colomar sign on your left. 'Colomar' in Catalan, or 'Palomar' in Spanish, means dovecote or pigeon house. Go left to make a short detour to **Colomar del Bertran**, medieval dovecote, then continue on the track for a few hundred metres and arrive at the ruins of **Castell del Serrat**.

The ruins of Castell de Serrat (Bertran)

Castell del Serrat (also known as Castell de Bertran) originates from the 11th century and was built on a great vantage point near the Muga river. Most of the buildings were built during the 13th century but it was most probably abandoned during the second half of the 15th century.

After visiting the ruins, retrace your steps to the **campsite**.

WALK 3
Beuda to El Mont

Start/finish	Beuda, village car park by the restaurant, N42.237066, E2.709016
Distance	11km
Total ascent/descent	850m
Grade	2
Time	4hr 20min, but allow some extra time to explore the ruins of the Castellot and the Sant Llorenç de Sous monastery
Refreshments	Restaurant in Beuda and on the summit of El Mont; spring by the monastery ruins and along the sealed road on the descent.
Access	Beuda is located 5km north of Besalú on the GIV-5234 road.
Public transport	Some buses from Besalú.

This occasionally very steep trail marked with yellow signs climbs El Mont from Beuda. En route you will pass the remains of Castellot perched on rocks and the ruins of the Sant Llorenç de Sous monastery. On a clear day your efforts will be rewarded with sweeping views of the diverse landscape.

It is easy to navigate through the handful of buildings that make up Beuda. From the village car park follow the yellow signs past the restaurant towards El Castellot. Walk across Plaça Major passing the 11th-century Sant Feliu de Beuda church and then continue alongside a picnic site and sports field with a large parking area. The ruins of Castellot on a rocky outcrop are visible from the village. Follow the tarmac road leaving Beuda. Ignore tracks on both sides and, when you see the El Castellot sign, leave the road to the left about 10min from the restaurant.

Follow the yellow signs through forest, passing the information board of El Castellot climbing school, and ignore the path on the left (marked as Sector Escalada). At **Camí de Ca n'Oliveres**, AG16 junction, keep left towards El Castellot. Ascend the narrow path through forest and shortly you have more views. Cross a rocky streambed and at Torrent de ca n'Oliveres, B1 junction, go left towards Castellot. Zigzag steeply uphill, and when the path splits the route

31

Mare de Déu
del Mont
El Mont ▲
1124m

Sant Llorenç de Sous

*Font de
Rocapastora*

Carr. de Mare de Deu del Mont

Turó de les Grives ✳

Castellot

Camí de Ca n'Oliveres

GIV-5234

Castell
de Beuda

SF

Beuda

GIV-5234

Montcal ▲

*Puig de
Cantallops* ▲

N

0   0.5
          km

continues straight on; however, first keep left uphill and a few minutes later reach the ruins of **Castellot**, where you can enjoy some stunning views towards Beuda.

> The **Castell de les Bruixes** (Castle of the Witches), also known as Castell dels Moros (Castle of the Moors), was built on a hilltop above Beuda, probably around 1000.
>
> In the Middle Ages the Queixàs family's Gothic castle of Beuda – located on the plains – became increasingly more influential in the area and it is believed that by 1285 the hilltop fort, Castellot, was abandoned.

From the ruins descend back to the junction and now go left. At Els Portals, B2 junction, go left uphill towards El Mont and Sant Llorenç de Sous (the timings on the signs are correct – you need an hour to cover 2km on very steep terrain). Zigzag uphill on the forest-covered mountainside. Shortly, notice a wooden sign, **Turó de les Grives**, on the left that marks a short detour to a rocky viewpoint.

Continue towards 'Sous' and ascend through the rock-scattered forest, followed by a very steep, rocky section. Follow the yellow signs and reach Sant Llorenç de Sous monastery about 30min from Els Portals. Explore the ruins and enjoy the views.

> The Benedictine **Sant Llorenç de Sous** monastery was first documented in 872 and it became an important monastery of the county of Besalú during the Romanesque period.
>
> Earthquakes in 1427 and 1429 damaged the buildings and after that it fell into disrepair.

Join the road behind the buildings by the **Sant Llorenç de Sous**, AG21, signpost, go left uphill and shortly after leave it to the right on a path marked with yellow and orange/green signs. Soon the views open up towards Besalú as you follow the narrow, rocky path on the mountainside. Reach a stone wall and then emerge on to a tarmac road about 20–25min from the monastery. Turn right and follow the road for a few minutes, and then – where the road bends left – leave it to the right on a path marked with yellow signs. Go through a gate and at Cursa Mitja Marató, MDM junction, follow the yellow signs straight on uphill. Shortly after, go through another gate and arrive at the summit of **El Mont** (alt. 1124m), the highest point in the area, which offers some fine views towards the higher mountains in the Pyrenees and the valleys below. The Catalan poet Jacint Verdaguer stayed in the sanctuary on the summit in 1884, and today his statue is located near the viewpoint. Here there is accommodation, and there are restaurants where you can dine before you start the descent: http://santuaridelmont.com.

Sculpture of Jacint Verdaguer i Santaló at the Santuari de la Mare de Déu del Mont

From the summit retrace your steps to the road by the monastery (about 30min). Go past the monastery and walk on the road for another 800 metres and reach **Font de Rocapastora**. Shortly after the spring look out for the path on the right marked with yellow signs. Take that path downhill towards Beuda.

As you zigzag downhill through the rock-scattered forest, occasionally there are views to Beuda, the valley and the nearby mountains. Descend on the rocky path, then on exposed rocks with views to a quarry near Beuda. El Castellot on the rocky outcrop also comes into view. Ignore any paths marked with 'X' and follow the yellow signs. Reach **Camí de Ca n'Oliveres**, AG16 junction, about an hour from the spring. Continue towards Beuda. When you reach the tarmac road go right and 10min later arrive back at the village.

WALK 4
Sadernes to Salt de Brull

Start/finish	Sadernes, N42.269465, E2.593738
Distance	17.5km
Total ascent/descent	780m
Grade	3
Time	5hr 30min–6hr
Refreshments	Café at Pont de Valentí; spring by the refuge.
Access	Sadernes is located on the GIV-5231 road, about 6km north of Montagut. Between April and November you have to pre-book your parking at the car park where the trail starts. The number of cars are limited but there are lots of spaces: www.turismegarrotxa.com.

The trail follows the rocky gorge of the Sant Aniol river, crossing it on stone bridges and stepping stones several times before arriving at the chapel of Sant Aniol d'Aguja. From the small chapel continue along the river to the Salt de Brull waterfall. Some sure-footedness might be required on the second part of the walk, which is more exposed.

Leave the car park by the Molí d'en Galzeran, G32 signpost. Descend on steps to the road and turn right. Shortly after, the sealed road becomes a gravel track passing a large field with a building. You might spot orange/green signs alongside the yellow signs.

After about 1km, cross a **bridge** and pass further parking areas along the track. (You need special permission to use these parking places.) The track snakes by a vertical rock wall which is very popular with climbers and the scenery is dominated by the rocky gorge. Walk across a small **bridge** and shortly after spot the café/hostel building in the gorge. At the G40 junction leave the track to the left on a path towards the hostel building. About 40–45min after leaving from Sadernes, cross the medieval bridge, **Pont de Valentí**. It was built on the access route to Sant Aniol chapel and was used by muleteers, coal men and smugglers. At the foot of the bridge keep right by the hostel building. Follow the yellow signs along the gorge. Ignore the unmarked paths heading down to the riverbank and stay on the well-trodden path among the trees. When the path splits go right downhill

Puig d'en Coll
1030m

Salt de Brull waterfall

Gorg Blau

Torrent de la Comella

Sant Aniol d'Aguja

El Tumany
841m

Cross the river
Stepping stones

Martanyà
1031m

Salt de la Núvia
Farmhouse

La Muntada

Riera de Sant Aniol

El Ferran
985m

Cross the river

Puig de Plansesserres
807m

Riera d'Escales

Pont de Valentí

Puig de Bistoltes
783m

Puig de Cofí
607m

N

Sadernes

P SF

GIV-5231

Riera d'Escales

0   1 km

towards Sant Aniol. From there, most junctions have a wooden signpost marking the direction and time to Sant Aniol. Reach and cross a track and continue on its other side, where the path bends slightly away from the gorge. The undulating rocky path gets close to and runs parallel to the track.

When you reach the track go left, pass some ruins and shortly after leave the track to the right. Cross the river on rocks. When the rocky path splits go left with the river on your left. Ignore any unmarked path or paths marked with 'X' and follow the yellow signs, passing a pile of sacks filled with building materials. You can volunteer to take a bag to the refuge building to help the restoration. Reach the riverbank at **La Muntada junction**. You will arrive back to this point from across the river (usually boots can stay on, but check the water level).

Go right on the rocky path by the rock wall towards Sant Aniol (according to the sign, it is still 50min away). Shortly after, cross the river on stepping stones and continue along the river on rocks. Soon you cross the river again, this time on rocks, and then walk among moss-covered trees. Go left by the signpost on the GR11 trail (Sadernes per Salt de la Núvia/Sant Aniol 15min). When the path splits follow the red/white signs to the left, ignore any unmarked path and reach a suspension bridge about 2hr from Pont de Valentí. Cross over and arrive at **Sant Aniol d'Aguja**.

> A **small monastery** was founded in 859 by a group of Benedictine monks. As it was built in a secluded area with few resources it never attracted a large religious community, and after 1003 it became a simple parish church. The single-nave, Romanesque building, covered with a barrel vault, dates back to the 11th century. The facade was rebuilt by soldiers after 1949 and a new bell was placed in the bell tower in 1962.

There is an old refuge building (under restoration at the time of writing) and a spring near the church. It is a popular place to stop for a picnic.

To continue to the Salt de Brull waterfall, take the path on the right behind the spring and follow it for about 20min. First pass **Gorg Blau**, an enticing rock pool with turquoise water, then climb over rocks, cross the river and continue hopping on rocks through the narrow gorge to arrive at the magnificent place where **Salt de Brull** cascades down to a rock pool.

From Salt de Brull retrace your steps to the spring by the refuge building and continue on the GR11 path towards Sadernes/Salt de la Núvia. Ascend through forest, passing some ruined stone houses. This section of the route is part of the GR11 long-distance trail, marked with red/white signs, but you can also see yellow and orange/green signs too. Shortly after the ruins, follow the exposed path with spectacular views to the nearby mountains and the gorge below.

Gorg Blau is a popular swimming spot along the route

About 45min from San Aniol d'Aguja, at **Salt de la Núvia**, G36 junction, go left downhill towards Sadernes. Descend through forest and soon you can spot a farmhouse in the valley. Zigzag steeply downhill and about 30min from the G36 junction arrive back to the river at **La Muntada**. Cross over, keep right and retrace your steps to Sadernes (about 1hr 10min away).

WALK 5
Volcà de Santa Margarida and Croscat

Start/finish	Can Blanc, Fageda d'en Jordà car park, N42.153843, E2.517915
Distance	12km
Total ascent/descent	350m
Grade	1
Time	3hr 30min
Refreshments	Kiosk at car park at the beginning; shop at La Fageda Cooperativa; drinking water at Sant Miquel church; café at Can Caselles; restaurants near Santa Margarida car park.
Access	Can Blanc is located about 3km outside of Olot along the GI-524 road; parking costs around €8 for a day (at time of going to print).
Public transport	Can Blanc is a few min bus ride from Olot Bus station.

This fascinating landscape, dotted with forest-covered volcanic hills is criss-crossed with several waymarked trails. Follow the well-trodden and well-signposted 'Ruta 1' that visits the hermitage of Santa Margarida, built in the crater of an extinct volcano, and then continue to the nearby Croscat Volcano.

From the car park take the underpass near the information building. Follow the path through beech forest and at the junction keep right towards Santa Margarida. Go left at the next junction. There are some houses and patches of fields near the path.

Follow the well-trodden path with signs towards Santa Margarida. At the junction continue straight on; the GR2 joins your route from the right for a short while. Pass a house, reach a track and go left, passing a transformer building. About 45min from the start reach a sealed road, keep right and shortly after pass the entrance of **La Fageda Cooperativa** (producing and selling dairy products). Follow the road that skirts around its buildings and pastures.

The scenery is dominated by volcanic cones, most covered with forest. Continue on a path after reaching the gate of Mas Prat de la Plaça farmhouse. At a signpost keep right uphill towards Santa Margarida.

Shortly after reach a sealed road near a house, go left and arrive at **Sant Miquel de Sacot Church**. From the church continue downhill alongside pastures, and a few minutes later reach a track and keep right downhill. Soon reach a sealed road by a volcanic rock with a cross and go right alongside a field. At the junction continue straight on uphill, passing further small pastures. At the next intersection go left towards Volcà Santa Margarida. At the signposted junction go left uphill. When you reach the rim of the volcano go left and keep right downhill by the next signpost, and then turn right downhill by the gate of Can Santa. The small hermitage in the middle of the crater comes into view as you descend. Reach the bottom of the crater about 30min from the Sant Miquel church. Walk to the **Hermitage of Santa Margarida** and then take the path behind the building. The crater is a popular picnic spot, as there is a path that leads there from the nearby Santa Margarida car park.

It is not certain why the 15th-century **Chapel of the Hermitage of Santa Margarida** was built in the crater of the volcano. The original chapel was destroyed by an earthquake around 1427, and the current building was built in 1865.

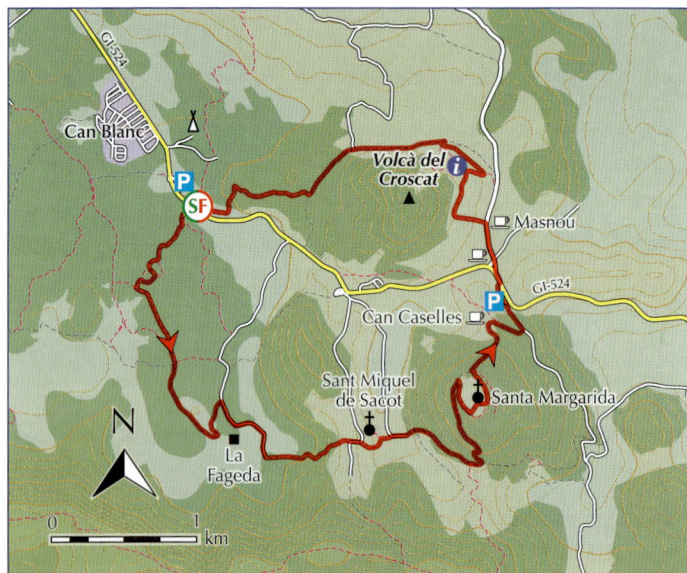

Climb some steps, and when you reach the rim keep right downhill. After a steep descent you have some views of the distant mountains. Pass a house, **Can Caselles**, that operates as La Volcanica café; its garden is dotted with interesting wooden sculptures. Carry straight on after the house, reach a track, go left and shortly after pass **Santa Margarida car park**. Cross the main road and go left parallel to the road, and 100 metres later go right towards Fageda d'en Jordà, passing a restaurant on the left and a turn-off to a campsite on the right. Pass a couple of buildings and when you reach a restaurant (Masnou) go left and head towards **Volcà del Croscat**. In a junction keep right and soon descend on steps and reach an information building. Follow the path that leads down to an exposed section of the volcano where you can see the volcanic layers.

The **Santa Margarida and Croscat Volcanoes** are the result of an eruption event some 11,500 years ago. The volcanoes were created by the volcanic eruption, which resulted from the interaction between water and magma (phreatomagmatic activity) alternating with magmatic activity when the magma pushes through cracks in the crust causing eruption.

Volcà del Croscat

The path then takes you up to a small viewpoint, and then back to the information building. Take the path on the left downhill and reach and then follow a track that skirts below the information building alongside fields. Meet a wide track and go left towards Fageda d'en Jordà. When you reach a sealed road keep left towards a gate and then left by a fence. Pass some buildings and then go right on a path as the sign-post indicates. At the junction near a ruined house go left through forest. Reach a track and go right, pass a house and arrive back at the **car park**.

WALK 6
Puig Rodó and Sant Miquel del Corb

Start/finish	Piscina Municipal (municipal swimming pool), Les Preses, N42.142891, E2.462503
Distance	13km
Total ascent/descent	850m
Grade	2
Time	5hr
Refreshments	Cafés and restaurants in Les Preses, water at picnic site.
Access	Les Preses is located along the C-152 road about 3km from Olot – you can park near the Piscina Municipal Les Preses.
Public transport	Buses from Girona and Olot to Les Preses.

This waymarked trail takes you to Puig Rodó, where you will be greeted by an impressive panorama of the Garrotxa Volcanic Zone and the high mountains of the Pyrenees beyond. The trail then continues through lush forest, first to Sant Martí Church and then to Sant Miquel del Corb Church, tucked away in the beech forest. The latter is one of the oldest churches in the Garrotxa.

Follow the yellow signs along Carrer Camp del Prat towards the Piscina Municipal, and then keep right at the fork and go alongside the fence of the municipal swimming pool. Shortly after, take the path on the right uphill towards Ermita St Miquel del Corb. There are some red/white GR signs, but your route is signposted with yellow markers. As you ascend through forest, ignore any unmarked paths or paths with an 'X'.

At Volcá del Racó, G143 junction, go right on Ruta de les Ermites de Corb. Shortly after, at **El Racó**, G144 junction, continue straight on uphill (you will return to this junction from the path on the left). Climb the rocky path through forest ignoring a path on the left.

Follow the yellow signs to the left by the signpost towards Àrea de Xenacs (20min). Soon walk on a tree-covered ridge. At the next junction go right towards Àrea de Xenacs, and – shortly after passing a viewpoint (Mirador de Xenacs) – arrive at the **Àrea de Xenacs picnic site**. Pass the building and car park, and at the P28 signpost continue downhill towards Mirador Puig Rodó. Ignore the first path

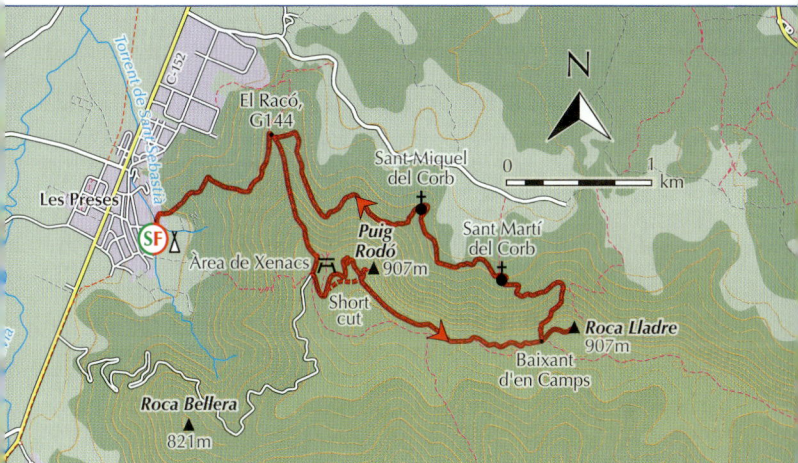

on the left marked 'Botanic Trail' and continue on the track, passing a charcoal burning site and a karst hole. Leave the track to the left on the second path marked 'Botanic Trail'. This narrow trail is dotted with plant names. (Alternatively just carry straight on and you will reach the junction where the path climbs to Puig Rodó. This route is just a few minutes shorter than the Botanic Trail.) About 15min

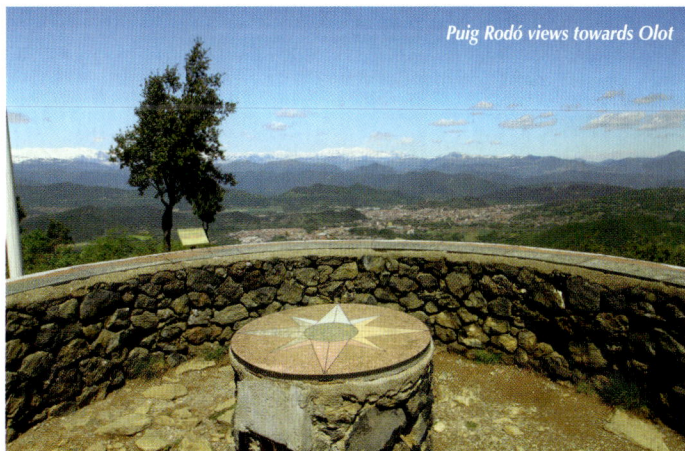

Puig Rodó views towards Olot

after joining the 'Botanic Trail', at a junction, take the first path on the left, which leads you to the viewpoint on **Puig Rodó** (alt. 907m). (The shortcut mentioned above joins this from the right.)

Enjoy the impressive panorama of the Garrotxa Volcanic Zone; there are views towards Olot and Les Preses, and on a clear day you can see all the way to the higher mountains of the Pyrenees. From the viewpoint return to the junction, go left and continue on a narrow forest path towards Serra del Corb. Pass Font del Cingles and at the junction with a signpost go left towards Fontpobra. A few minutes later keep left on the path marked with a yellow sign. Follow the path on the hillside through forest for about 10min and go left at the next junction. Descend to **Baixant d'en Camps**, G77 junction, and turn left downhill towards Les Preses (pel Corbs). To continue to **Roca Lladre** (alt. 907m) for further views follow the unmarked path straight on. From Roca Lladre return to G77 junction and go right.

Zigzag downhill on the often very steep path for about 40min, ignoring any unmarked path or path marked with an 'X', and arrive at **Ermita de Sant Martí del Corb**. The small Romanesque church with single nave and semicircular apse is located in the forest near a large farmhouse.

Go past the church and continue on the track straight on. Reach a farm building, go left and in 10min arrive at **Sant Miquel del Corb Church**, one of the oldest churches in the Garrotxa.

> The **Sant Miquel del Corb** is a single-nave church with a barren vault. It was built in a Romanesque style, but it also shows some signs of Pre-Romanesque origins and was rebuilt in the 18th century.

From the church continue on the wide path ignoring a path on the left. It soon becomes a narrow forest path on the mountainside. Here you can see red/white GR signs alongside the yellow signs. Pass Font de Racó. Keep right downhill by the fence and skirt below some houses following the yellow signs. Reach **El Racó**, G144 junction, go right and retrace your steps to **Les Preses** (1km).

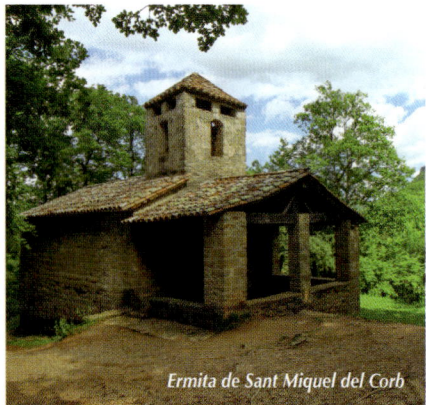

Ermita de Sant Miquel del Corb

WALK 7
Salt de la Coromina and Camí Ral

Start/finish	Els Hostalets d'en Bas village car park, N42.103282, E2.452443
Distance	11km
Total ascent/descent	550m
Grade	2
Time	3hr 30min
Refreshments	Cafés and restaurants in Hostalets d'en Bas.
Access	Hostalets d'en Bas is located along the GIP-5272 road off the C-153 road south of Olot.
Public transport	www.vallbas.cat/municipi/tad/ – on-demand bus in the Bas Valley.

This route climbs above the picturesque village of Els Hostalets d'en Bas, with some great views towards Puigsacalm and the nearby mountains around the Bas Valley. Admire the impressive Salt de la Coromina waterfall before descending on a well-preserved section of the historic trading route, Camí Ral, through dense forest.

From the large car park that is located just outside the village, follow the road into the 18th-century village built on the fertile land of the Bas Valley. Walk through the main street lined with charming traditional houses, cafés and restaurants. Keep left on Plaça Major in front of the **Santa Maria Church**, and shortly after – at **Els Hostalets d'en Bas**, G65 junction – go right towards Falgars.

Follow the narrow road alongside fields towards the houses, ignoring a track on the right and passing **Font de la Clapera**. Pass some farmhouses and the track comes to an end at Els Terrers (a group of houses). Reach the stream by the wooden sign 'Falgars' and cross over on rocks. Continue on the other side uphill. A few minutes later when the path splits, follow the yellow signs to the right through forest. Shortly after, reach a sealed road and keep right uphill, following it for about 60 metres, then leave it to the right on a path. Zigzag uphill on the occasionally steep path following the yellow markers on the forested mountainside. Reach and cross a track, and continue to climb the narrow path on its other side.

Emerge on to a sealed road, keep right and a few metres later leave it to the left and follow the yellow signs. Shortly after, reach the sealed road again and go left uphill on the road. As the road winds its way uphill, you have some great views of the mountains surrounding the Bas Valley.

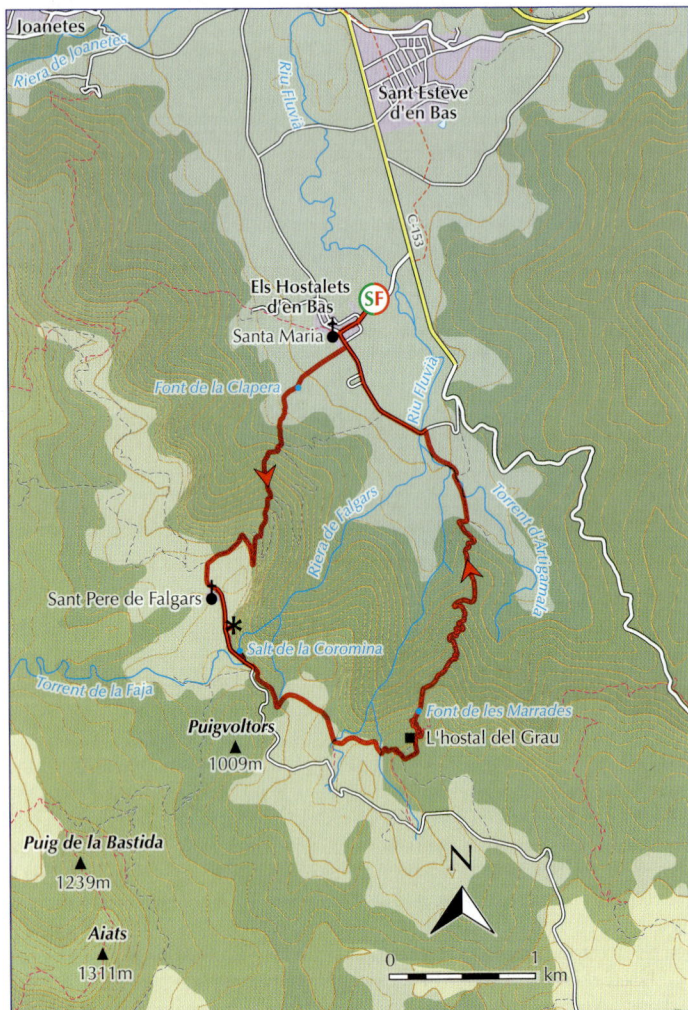

Els Hostalets d'en Bas and its rapeseed meadows

Go through a gate near a farmhouse, and at the signpost continue straight on. Follow the road alongside fields to Falgars, a group of houses with a church, **Sant Pere de Falgars**. You can also see some red/white GR signs on this section. Shortly after passing Falgars – about 1hr 20min from Els Hostalets d'en Bas – look out for the waterfall, **Salt de la Coromina**, cascading below you on your left.

Continue on the road and soon cross the river that feeds the waterfall. Follow the yellow signs to the left, leaving the road by an electricity post. Descend on the path and go through a gate. When the path splits, follow the yellow signs to the right and then across the meadow. Cross the river and go through a gate and then keep left on a path. At a small clearing keep sharply right downhill. Go through another gate, drop down to the riverbank and cross over on rocks.

Ascend for a short distance and at the path junction go left. Shortly after at **L'hostal del Grau**, G68 junction, go left towards Els Hostalets d'en Bas. Pass a gate, cross a track, go through a gate and walk alongside a field. Shortly after go through another gate and then skirt around L'hostal del Grau. Join the old Camí Ral transport route and descend through forest, passing a memorial and – shortly after – a spring, **Font de les Marrades**.

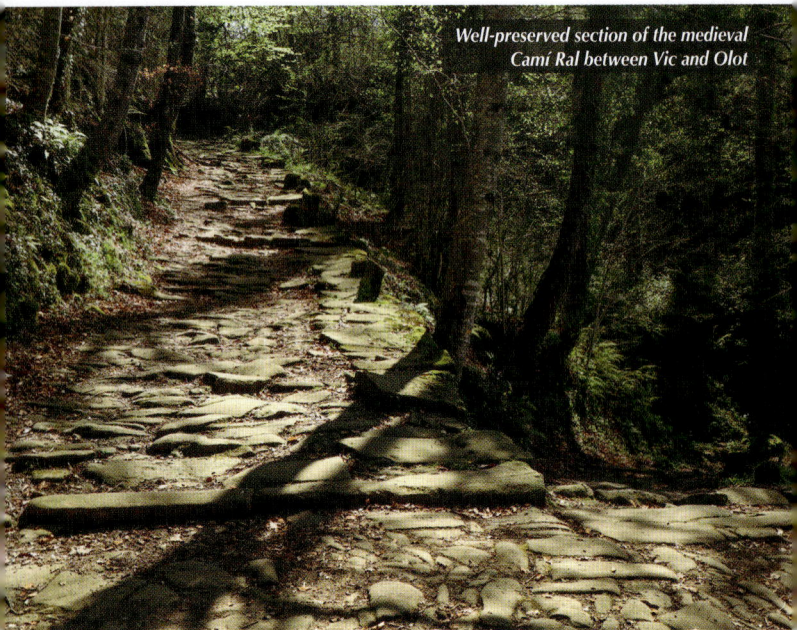

Well-preserved section of the medieval Camí Ral between Vic and Olot

Inns provided food and accommodation for travellers passing along the medieval road, **Camí Ral**, which was used to transport goods between Olot and Vic. More and more lodgings were built in the most prominent area of the road, and this developed into the small village of Els Hostalets d'en Bas.

At the junction go left downhill and soon you can spot some yellow signs. At the next junction go right and through a gate, and then descend through forest. Reach a track by L'esquirol Casa Rural (rural accommodation) and turn left. Cross a river on the bridge by a house and keep left on the path. Walk alongside fields and reach a tarmac road, then go left crossing the **El Fluvia river**. Follow the road alongside fields back to the village and then to the car park.

WALK 8
Puigsacalm from Joanates

Start/finish	Joanates, N42.121255, E 2.417237
Distance	11km
Total ascent/descent	1120m
Grade	3+
Time	6hr–6hr 30min
Refreshments	None along the way.
Access	Joanates is located on the GIV-5273 road, about 5km from Les Preses. The starting point is 250 metres west of the church in the village, just before that road joins the main road. You can park along the road on this section.
Public transport	Some buses from Olot.

This full-day walk takes in the rocky outcrop, Puig dels Llops, as well as the popular Puigsacalm and provides some far-reaching views along the way. This is an exciting but demanding route with some scrambling up the narrow Canal Fosca and then during the descent through Canal dels Ganxos Vells. Only attempt to follow this route in dry weather.

Take the path towards Santa Magdalena pel Barret (1hr 30min) and pass a couple of houses. Follow the narrow path marked with yellow signs uphill passing two more houses. Walk, initially among shrubs and then on rocks, ignoring any unmarked paths or paths marked with 'X'. Keep left by the tin sign towards Santa Magdelena per Sacarena. Zigzag steeply uphill through forest and you get the first glimpse of the nearby mountains at around 1km. The foliage occasionally opens up and you can stop to catch your breath and enjoy some views.

After around 45min, climb for around 1.5km and a vertical rock face comes into sight. Head towards it through shrubs ignoring any other paths. You are accompanied by some views towards Les Preses, Olot and Joanates. When the path splits by a big slab of rock (**El Barret**), take the path on the right (you will return to this junction from the left). The scrambling starts almost immediately. Climb on rocks and then shortly after ascend on some iron steps as you scramble through the gully, Canal Fosca. There are some aided sections with chains to hold on to, but it is not a via ferrata route and you can scramble up without any special equipment. After a scramble of about 30min, reach a path and shortly after emerge on to a meadow.

Turn right (there is an antenna with a building on the left) and descend on the grassy path for a few minutes to reach **Santa Magdelena del Mont Church**.

The **hermitage** was first documented in 998. The church was modified during the 18th century, but the apse and the semicircular vault of the primitive Romanesque church remains. Next to the church the old farmhouse operates as a refuge.

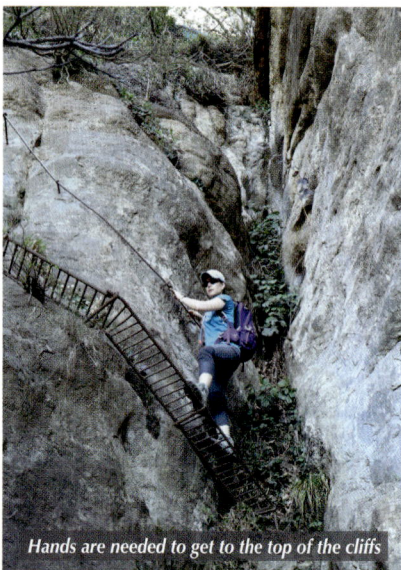

Hands are needed to get to the top of the cliffs

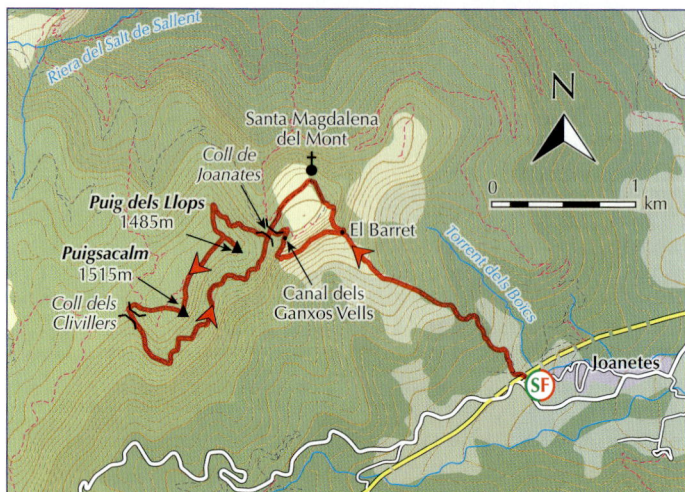

Santa Magdalena del Mont and views to the Pyrenees

You can admire the views towards the mountains of the Pyrenees. Facing the church keep left and follow the wide grassy path. The spring, Font de Santa Magdelena, is on the right-hand side of the path, but it is no more than dripping water. At Santa Magdalena del Mont, G61 junction, go left uphill on a rocky path towards Puigsacalm. A few minutes later reach a narrow path and keep right towards the towering rock face with views of the mountains.

At the junction with the signpost take the Puigsacalm pel Puig dels Llops route to the right (you will return to this junction from the left on the Puigsacalm pel dels Burros route). Ascend the narrow path through forest, and farther on there are some views towards the Pyrenees on your right.

The path widens as you head towards Puig dels Llops. In a path junction keep left to climb the rocky peak of **Puig dels Llops** (alt. 1485m), where you are greeted with a 360-degree panorama. The nearby Puigsacalm dominates the immediate landscape. Down below you can see Olot and Les Preses, while to the north you can see the Pyrenees, and on a clear day you can make out the mountains of the Montseny Massif in the distance.

From the peak descend back to the last junction and carry straight on towards the next peak, Puigsacalm (you came from the path on the right) with views

51

The rocky outcrop of Puig dels Llops with Olot in the distance

towards the Pyrenees on your right. When the path splits, continue straight on and climb the well-trodden path to the peak of **Puigsacalm** (alt. 1515m). There are views to the rocky outcrop, Puig dels Llops. You can make out Olot and Les Preses down below; the Pyrenees mountains dominate the north and on a clear day you can make out the forked peaks of the iconic Pedraforca to the west.

From the peak descend the (other) well-trodden path to the west to Puigsacalm junction with a signpost. Go left towards Sta. Magdalena pel Pas dels Burros and a few minutes later, at the big junction with a signpost, go left downhill on a path marked Santa Magdalena pel Pas dels Burros. First descend steeply downhill and then along a rocky ledge with views. At the junction with several signs take the Camí pel Pas dels Burros route to the left. For about 45min follow the narrow path that initially skirts just below Puigsacalm and Puig dels Llops and then follows a rocky mountainside with some great views.

At the junction with the signpost (you took the path on the left on the way to Puig dels Llops) go right and then a few metres later keep right again. Follow the narrow path for about 150 metres and then look out for and turn right on to a steep narrow path. Scramble down on rocks for about 30min. Some sections are steep and are aided with iron steps and iron chains. Follow the ledge and reach the path junction, **El Barret**, where there is a slab of rock. Go right downhill and descend for about 40min back to **Joanates**.

WALK 9

Puigsacalm from Coll de Bracons

Start/finish	Coll de Bracons, N42.108394, E2.376392
Distance	9km (there and back)
Total ascent/descent	420m
Grade	2
Time	3hr
Refreshments	None
Access	Coll de Bracons is located on the GIV-5273 road approximately 6km west from Joanates; there is space to park along the road but – since it is a popular route to Puigsacalm – arrive early and try to avoid weekends.

This popular there-and-back route takes you to the peak of Puigsacalm, where a stunning 360-degree panorama greets you. It is a shorter and easier route than the trail described in Walk 8; however, you can extend your day by continuing to the nearby Puig dels Llops.

The snow-capped mountains of the Pyrenees are visible in the distance

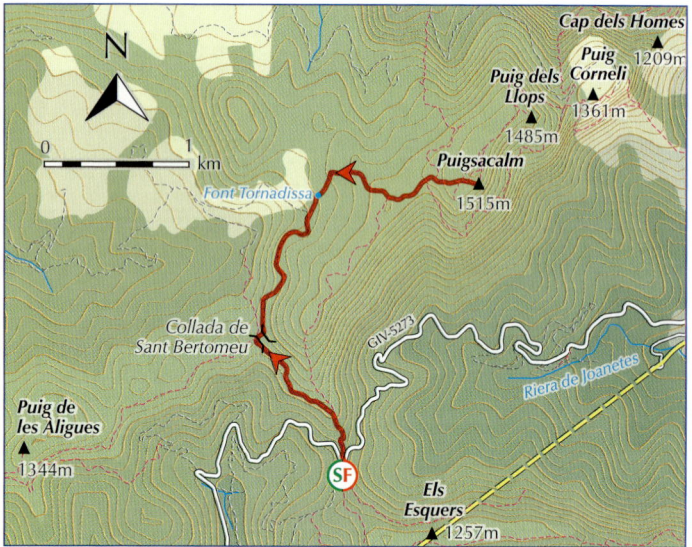

Opposite the information board climb up on rocks from the GIV-5273 road. There are yellow signs that you can follow all the way to Puigsacalm. Follow the yellow signs on the well-trodden path through beech forest ignoring any paths marked with an 'X'. Reach **Collada de Sant Bertomeu** after about 30min and carry on following the yellow markers. Pass **Font Tornadissa** about 1hr into the walk and cross a stream on rocks. Emerging from the forest climb the grassy hillside. Cross a track at the top and, when the path splits, follow the yellow signs straight on uphill. You can enjoy some views towards the Pyrenees. At Els Rasos de Manter go right towards Puigsacalm, keeping just slightly above the wide track.

At the Ras de les Oivaderes junction keep left and go through a gate. Less than 10min later arrive at a big junction with several waymarkers. Carry straight on towards Santa Magdalena pel Puig dels Llops and a few minutes later at the Puigsacalm signposted junction go right uphill on the stony path and make the final steep climb to **Puigsacalm** (alt. 1515m). Enjoy the 360-degree views to the higher mountains of the Pyrenees as well as the nearby Puig dels Llops, and on a clear day you can see the mountains of the Montseny Massif and even Pedraforca in the distance. From the peak descend back to Puigsacalm junction from where you can go right and continue to Puig dels Llops (optional) before you retrace your steps to Coll de Bracons.

WALK 10
Salt de Sallent

Start/finish	Car park, Sant Privat d'en Bas, N42.149236, E2.409161
Distance	12km
Total ascent/descent	700m
Grade	2
Time	4hr 30min
Refreshments	None
Access	From Olot take C-152 to Les Preses and from there go west on GIP-5226 road to Sant Privat d'en Bas.
Public transport	www.vallbas.cat/municipi/tad/ – on-demand bus in the Bas Valley.

The route climbs through lush forest, which is home to wild garlic in the spring, to the waterfall Salt de Sallent. The trail described traverses just above the waterfall with views to the Bas Valley and then descends to the gorge, crossing the river on rocks several times.

From the car park, heading towards the houses, go towards Salt de Sallent. Go through the archway and then across Plaça Major to the **church**. At Sant Privat d'en Bas, G151 junction, turn left towards Joanates.

Leaving the houses at the junction keep right uphill, and shortly after leave the road to the left on a narrow path. Go through a gate passing Can Valencia and then follow the track alongside a fence. At La Canova Riu Gurn, G57 junction, keep left, go through a gate and drop down to the river and cross over on a **footbridge**. Keep right passing some buildings. When you reach a road, turn right and follow it, ignoring a track that leads to the Els Pins picnic site on the right. Pass the **picnic site** and some parking places (this can be an alternative starting point). At **Pla d'en Xurri**, G58 junction, continue straight on towards Salt de Sallent (the time on the sign refers to your return route). Pass some further parking areas and a barrier, ignoring a track on the left. About 50 metres after the barrier leave the track to the left towards Salt de Sallent pel Camí dels Matxos. Follow the yellow signs uphill through forest ignoring any paths marked with an 'X'.

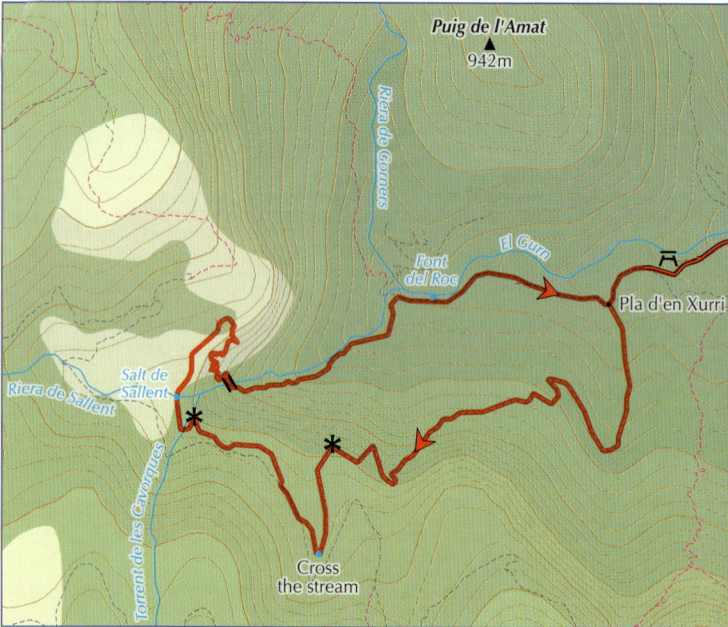

Puig de l'Amat
942m

Riera de Gorners

Font
del Roc

El Gurn

Pla d'en Xurri

Salt de
Sallent

Riera de Sallent

Torrent de les Cavorgues

Cross
the stream

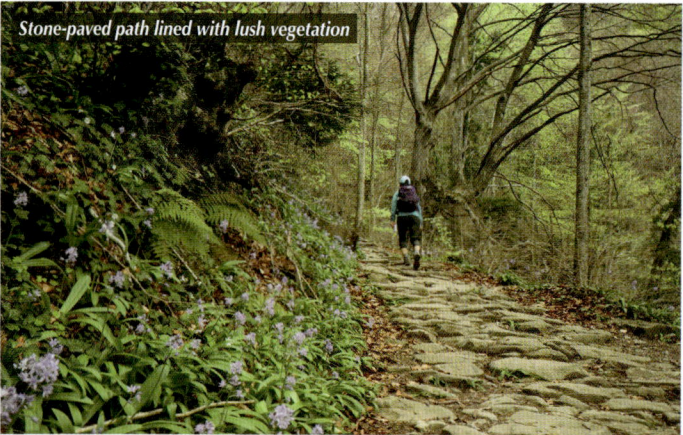

Stone-paved path lined with lush vegetation

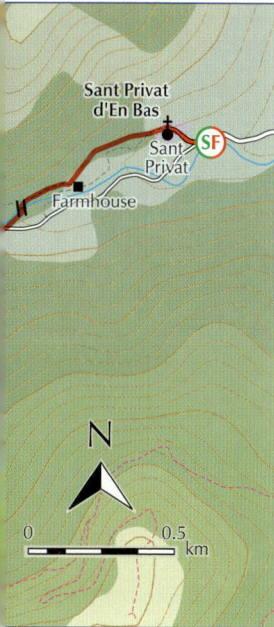

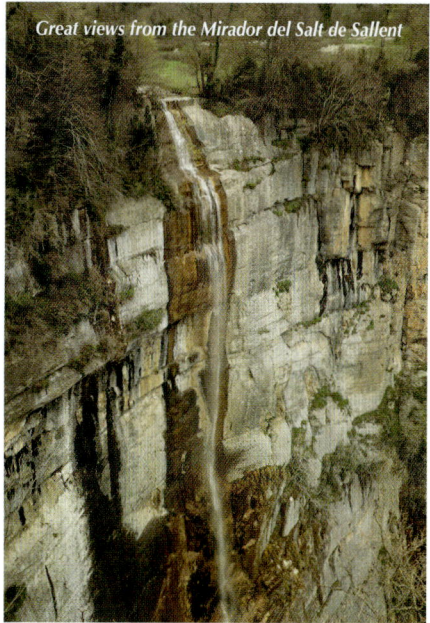
Great views from the Mirador del Salt de Sallent

The lush forest is scattered with boulders and soon you ascend on the 'paved' Camí de Maixos. Cross a rocky riverbed (Torrent dels Xerrics) and then shortly after you have some views to the nearby mountains and towards Sant Privat d'en Bas. The sound of trickling water often accompanies you as you climb the rocky path. **Cross the stream** (Torrent del Ginebrar) on rocks. After nearly an hour on this path, reach a track at Els Restobles, G56 junction.

Turn right for Salt de Sallent (15min) and about 150 metres later leave the track to the right on an unmarked narrow path among shrubs. Descend slightly on this rocky footpath which takes you to the **viewpoint** where you can admire the water cascading down on rocks. (However, there are better views awaiting you on the other side.) From the viewpoint continue on the footpath and cross Torrent de les Cavorques on rocks. Shortly after cross the Riera de Sallent on rocks just above the **Salt de Sallent waterfall**, but keep well away from the edge. Don't attempt to cross during or after heavy rain or if the water level is high or fast flowing! There are some great views of the Bas Valley towards Sant Privat d'en Bas, Olot and the mountains beyond.

The route back runs along the river Sallent

At the junction with a signpost go right, leaving the route marked with yellow signs towards Sant Privat, and then through a gate. This path is marked with a yellow 'X'. Descend on the narrow, rocky and often steep path, which has some dramatic views to the waterfall. There are some steps as you are getting closer to the waterfall. Reach a junction with wooden signs and take a detour to a vantage point (Mirador de Sota el Sallent) to the right. It is possible to descend a bit further down for more views.

Return to the path junction with wooden signs and continue downhill (if you took the detour, it is the path on the right). There are some iron staples in the rocks and ropes to help the steep descent. Reach and cross the river on a **footbridge** and continue on its other side. Shortly after, cross another stream on rocks and then descend for about 15–20min in the lush gorge with water rushing down on rocks near the path. There are some circular green markers with a walker symbol. After crossing a stream on rocks reach a track and go right, passing **Font del Roc** (spring). Ignore a track on the right and shortly after notice the path on the right towards Salt de Sallent pel Camí dels Matxos. Continue on the track and retrace your steps to the picnic site or to **Sant Privat d'en Bas**.

Oix to Santa Maria d'Escales

Start/finish	Oix, N42.269551, E2.528884
Distance	12.5km
Total ascent/descent	450m
Grade	2
Time	4hr
Refreshments	None along the way.
Access	Oix is located along the GIV-5221 road about 10km north from Castellfollit de la Roca; there is a large car park just outside Oix near the football pitch and playground, by Riera d'Oix.
Public transport	Buses from Olot.

From the small village of Oix this signposted trail crosses the rocky gorge and then climbs the narrow path dotted with mysterious ruins to the charming Santa Maria d'Escales church. Views are dominated by the rocky gorge and mountains, and the route crosses the Roman Bridge as it returns to the village.

From the parking area follow the road skirting around the football pitch towards the village. There is another (smaller) car park near the **Sant Llorenç Church**. Follow the GIV-5221 road leaving the houses of Oix and then, about 800 metres from the church, leave the road to the right on a gravel road towards Vall d'Hortmoier. Pass **Can Pei** guest house.

Shortly after, the track runs alongside the rocky gorge, signposted with yellow/white signs and yellow signs. Ignore any unmarked path or paths marked with an 'X'. Follow the track with views dominated by the surrounding mountains for about 30min to **Pont Trencat**, Mi04 junction. Continue straight on over the bridge and, just after the bridge at the Mi05 junction, keep right downhill towards Mare de Déu d'Escales. Descend on the narrow path ignoring a path on the right. Pass some ruins and follow the yellow signs to the bottom of the rocky gorge with the river. Walk on rocks and cross over on a small bridge, then ascend on a narrow path through forest. Passing the ruins of a building, climb the rocky path and then follow a ridge with some views of the surrounding mountains and river below.

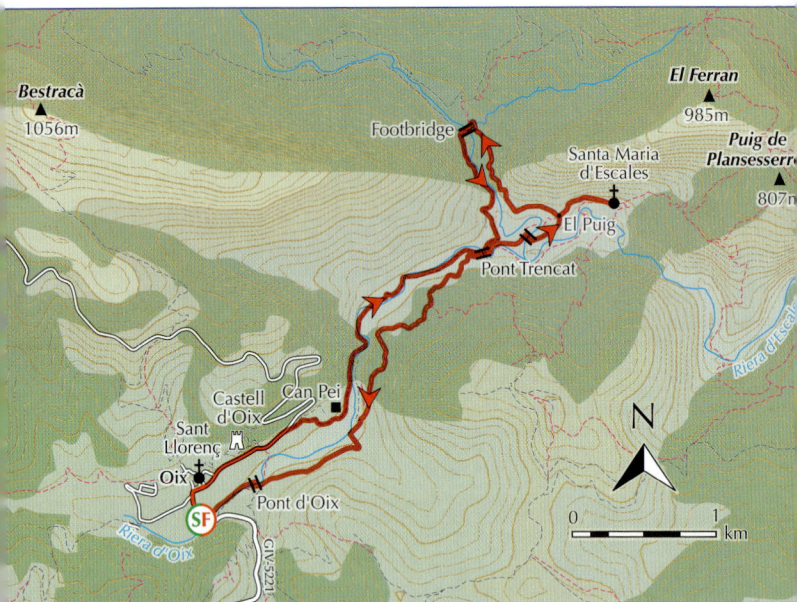

At **El Puig**, Mi06 junction, go right downhill towards Mare de Déu d'Escales (you will return to this junction from the church). Follow the narrow path mostly downhill for about 15min. When the path splits keep left and reach the **Church of Maria d'Escales**.

The church of **Santa Maria d'Escales** was first documented in 977 and has been mentioned in several documents throughout the centuries. The facade of the single-nave Romanesque church showcases different phases of the construction; some parts were built as recently as the 17th century.

Just like many other churches in the area, it was looted in 1936, and the restoration work was started in 1976 by the Friends of the Alta Garrotxa.

From Mare de Déu d'Escales climb back to **El Puig**, Mi06 junction, and keep right towards Pas dels Lliberals. Almost immediately ignore a path marked with an 'X' on the left. Follow the narrow rocky path uphill with views of the nearby mountains and the gorge of the snaking Riera de Beget below. Shortly after, the path drops down by a rock wall and then you walk among moss-covered trees.

Church of Santa Maria d'Escales

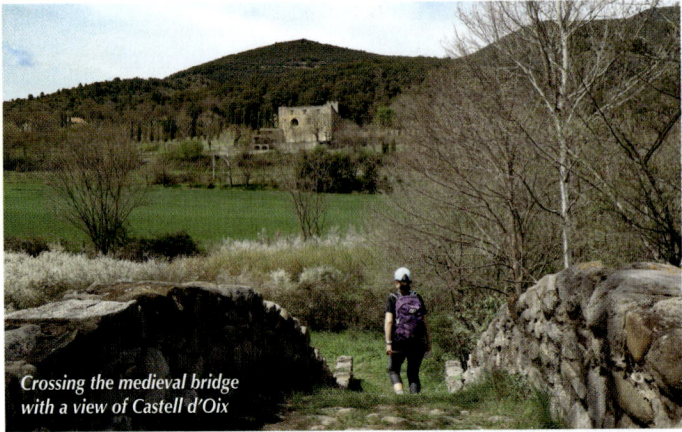

Crossing the medieval bridge with a view of Castell d'Oix

At La Palanca del Samsó, Mi07 junction, go left downhill towards Oix. This section is part of a GR trail, therefore you can see red/white stripes as well as yellow signs. After about 30–35min of descent from El Puig, Mi06 junction, pass a stone bridge overgrown by ivy, head towards the long **footbridge** and cross over Riera de Beget. At La Plantada, AG8 junction, go left towards Oix, through a gate with a cattle grid and continue on the track. You can spot the footpath you descended earlier on the mountainside across the river. When the track splits, go left and descend the stony track back to the Mi05 junction. Go right and cross **Pont Trencat bridge** again.

Just after the bridge at Pont Trencat, Mi04 junction, go left towards Oix Pont Roman. At a clearing follow the yellow signs to the left uphill and then cross a riverbed and descend. At Pla d'en Pei, AG14 junction, go right downhill towards Oix (30min), pass a farmhouse and cross a streambed. Reach a track and go left. Cross the field and then keep right on a narrow path alongside pastures. Turn right on a path as the yellow marker indicates. Soon you begin to walk alongside fields, and you can see the 15th-century Castell d'Oix and the village in the distance. Pass a house and continue on a track, then leave it to the right on a path marked with yellow signs and arrive at the bridge, **Pont d'Oix**. Cross the bridge and continue alongside the river. Shortly after, arrive back at the car park at the edge of **Oix**.

Pont d'Oix is known as the Roman Bridge; however, the construction is only from the Romanesque period. It is, however, highly possible that there was an existing bridge well before that.

WALK 12
Castell de Besora

Start/finish	Car park at Castell de Montesquiu, N42.111990, E2.212224
Distance	10km
Total ascent/descent	490m
Grade	2
Time	3hr
Refreshments	Drinking water at the start; none on the way.
Access	Montesquiu is located 12km south of Ripoll along the C-17 road. From the village cross the River Ter on its only bridge and enter Parc del Castell de Montesquiu. Follow the road for about 1km snaking up to the car park.
Public transport	Buses from Ripoll to Montesquiu.

The waymarked SL-C 129 route connects two castles: Castell de Montesquiu and Castell de Besora. The forest tracks are easy to follow and you are often accompanied by far-reaching views. Allow some time to explore the ruins of Castell de Besora, perched on rocks overlooking the village of Santa Maria de Besora and the surrounding mountains.

Take the paved track by the wall of the castle grounds and pass a picnic site (Àrea d'esplai de la font del Castell Xic). When the track splits after the picnic site, take the left branch towards Santa Maria de Besora/Castell de Besora. Ignore a track on the right and follow the green/white signs straight on slightly uphill and shortly pass a concrete **reservoir**. The track splits after the reservoir, take the right branch (you are returning to this junction from the left). Alongside the SL-C 129 green/white signs you can see some red/white signs marking the GR151 route. A few minutes later go through a barrier and continue straight on uphill.

When the track splits, keep right. On a clear day there are views all the way to the mountains of the Montseny Massif on the right. Shortly after, leave the track by the signpost to the right on a path towards Castell de Besora. Walk alongside a field. Heading towards a building, cross the meadow and locate a signpost near the old **abandoned farmhouse**. Soon the ruins of the castle perched on rocks come into sight.

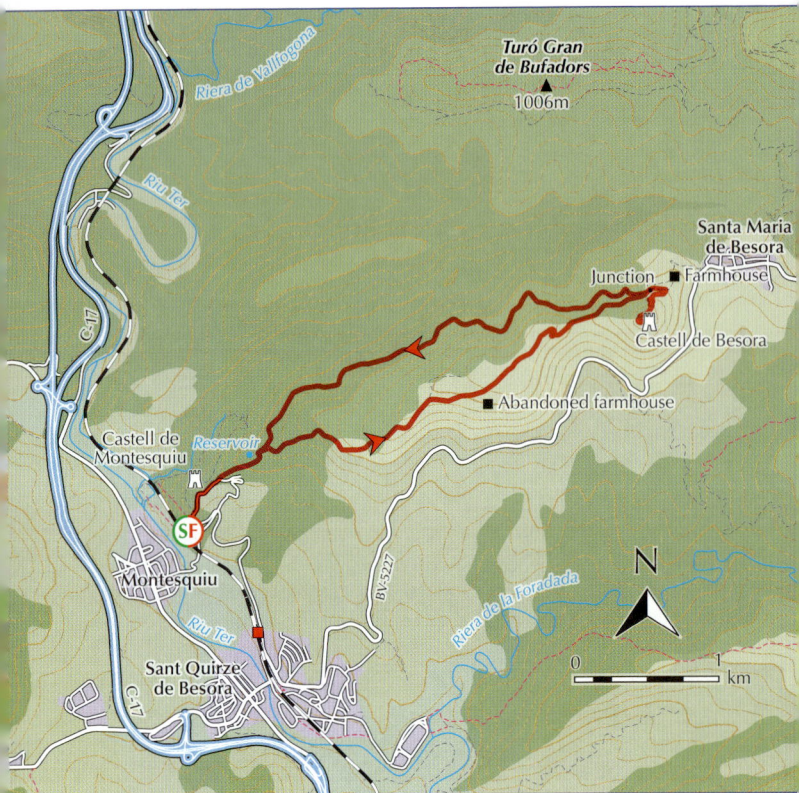

Walk alongside fields and pastures on the plateau and then the path drops down to the mountainside. Traverse the narrow, rocky, grey ridge leading towards the ruins. It seems that you would reach the castle shortly; however, the trail skirts below the ruins through forest before the final climb. Reach a **junction** and notice a wide path turning sharply left (you will return to this junction and to Montesquiu via that path). However, at first ignore a grassy track on the left and follow the wide track along a fence that bends right alongside fields. Near the farm, follow the signs to the right uphill towards the castle. Shortly after, walk through forest again with some views towards the village of Santa Maria de Besora. Zigzag uphill through the dense forest and reach the ruins of **Castell de Besora**.

The **Castell de Besora** was first mentioned in 895 and the church of Santa Maria was documented in 898. By the 17th century the castle was already decaying, and today only the remains of the walls and the church are visible.

The church was rebuilt several times over the centuries, and the portal and the circular window of the western wall were built in 1590. It was the parish church until 1759, when a new parish church was built below at Pla de Teia.

There are views towards the mountains of Montseny range and on a clear day you can make out the forked peaks of the iconic Pedraforca in the distance.

From the ruins retrace your steps through forest to the junction by the **farm**. Keep left along the fence and arrive back at the junction that you passed earlier and take the forest path following the green/white signs. The path then becomes a forest track. Follow it for about 30min mostly downhill before emerging at the junction near the concrete **reservoir**. Go right and retrace your steps to the car park.

Views from Castell de Besora

Eroded ridge heading towards Castell de Besora

The fortified building of **Castell de Montesquiu** was first documented in 1285 and, with the castles of Besora and Saderre, it formed part of a defensive line. During the Middle Ages it was used by the lords of the nearby Besora castle. The castle was then rebuilt during the 17th and 19th centuries. Since 1972 it has belonged to the Council of Barcelona, and today it is the headquarters of the Parc del Castell de Montesquiu, which was created in 1986.

For opening times and guided tours visit www.osonaturisme.cat/what-to-do/ natural-spaces-and-landscape/parc-del-castell-de-montesquiu.

WALK 13
Gorg de Masica

Start/finish	Vallfogana de Ripollès, N42.194888, E2.303567
Distance	11km (there and back)
Total ascent/descent	500m
Grade	1
Time	4hr–4hr 30min
Refreshments	Café/restaurant in Vallfogana de Ripollès; none along the way.
Access	Vallfogana de Ripollès is located along the N-260a road, 12km east of Ripoll; there is a car park at the south end of the village at the junction of Camí Meridià Verd and Plaça de la Vila.
Public transport	Buses from Ripoll and Olot to Vallafogana de Ripollès.

From the charming village of Vallfogana de Ripollès descend to a medieval bridge and take this comfortable there-and-back route which allows you to enjoy some spectacular waterfalls in a lush gorge. It is an easy route; however, with countless fantastic photo opportunities and great picnic spots, it can quickly turn into a full-day outing.

From the car park at the south side of the village descend towards Castell de Milany to a **medieval bridge**. There are some purple circle signs to follow. After crossing the medieval bridge (Pont Medieval) keep left by the river at the junction. Follow the narrow path alongside the river for a few minutes. Cross the river on a **footbridge** and keep right alongside the river (it is on your right). When you reach the sealed road, follow it to the right alongside fields, ignoring a track on the right. When the road forks, take the right gravel branch towards Castell de Milany. There are some houses on the other side of the river on your right.

When you come to an information board about the mountain ranges of the local area (Milany, Santa Magdalena and Puigsacalm-Bellmunt), look out for the narrow path on the left, which you can follow for about 200 metres to a kiln (**Teuleria del Pinetar**), and which also takes you closer to the waterfall. From the kiln return to the track and continue, passing **Font de la Tosca**.

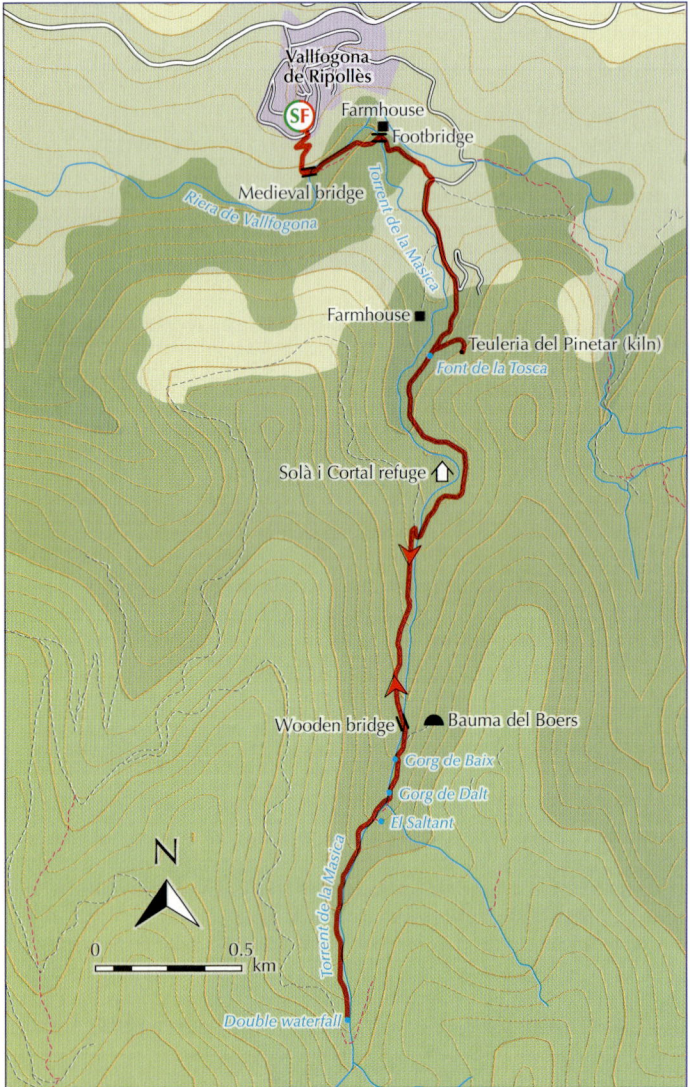

Vallfogona
de Ripollès

SF

Farmhouse

Footbridge

Medieval bridge

Riera de Vallfogona

Torrent de la Mística

Farmhouse

Teuleria del Pinetar (kiln)

Font de la Tosca

Solà i Cortal refuge

Wooden bridge
Bauma del Boers

Gorg de Baix

Gorg de Dalt

El Saltant

N

0   0.5
|___|___|___|
          km

Torrent de la Mística

Double waterfall

Soon you can spot the old forest refuge building, **Solà i Cortal**, down by the river. Ignore a track on the right and stay on the track, crossing the Torrent de la Masica in the bend. About 10–15min from Font de la Tosca leave the track to the left on a narrow path up the steps by the Masica Stream information board. There you can spot blue circle signs. Ignore the path on the right with a wooden sign saying 'Barraca d'en Buixate', which leads to the remains of a stone building. Continue on the narrow path marked with a blue circle with the river on your left. There are several paths heading down to the river, but stay on the well-trodden path through forest. At the path junction go left towards Torrent-Bauma del Boer. Shortly after, cross a **wooden bridge** and continue on the other side of the river. Before long you reach the first waterfall, **Gorg de Baix**.

El Saltant waterfall

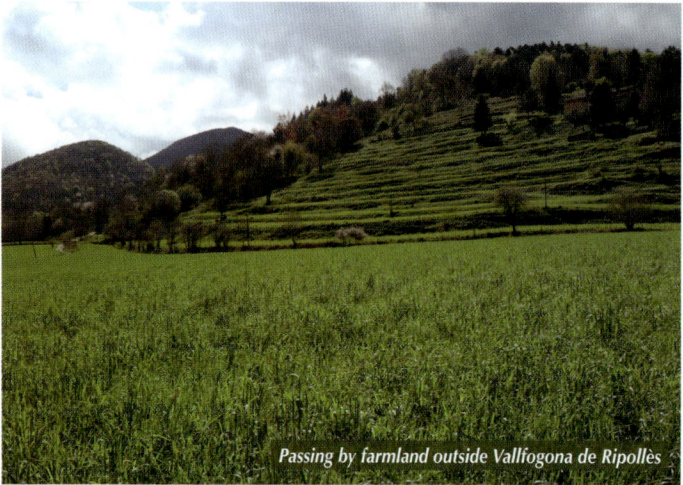

Passing by farmland outside Vallfogona de Ripollès

From the waterfall climb the steps, and at the junction go right towards **Gorg de Dalt** (100 metres). After the waterfall rejoin the path and continue on the narrow path with the river on your right. Shortly after, cross the river on rocks and reach the next waterfall, **El Saltant**. Ascend and at the junction go left (Antic camí de carreta de Llastanosa a la Barraca 2km).

At the junction with the information board go right and continue with the river on your left. There are several paths marked with a camera symbol leading closer to the river where you can take photos of other waterfalls. The path keeps close to the river and the constant sound of rushing water accompanies you. There are some green diamond markers on posts to follow as well. Reach another path and keep left with the river on your left. Ascend and cross the river on rocks. Shortly after, you can see the amazing **double waterfall** that marks your turnaround point. From the double waterfall retrace your steps to **Vallfogona de Ripollès**.

Vallfogona de Ripollès village was built in the 13th century when the lords of Milany wanted to have a community around La Sala Castle. The walled settlement was only accessible via three gates.

RIPOLLÈS

Walkers heading towards Refugi de Coma de Vaca (Walk 26)

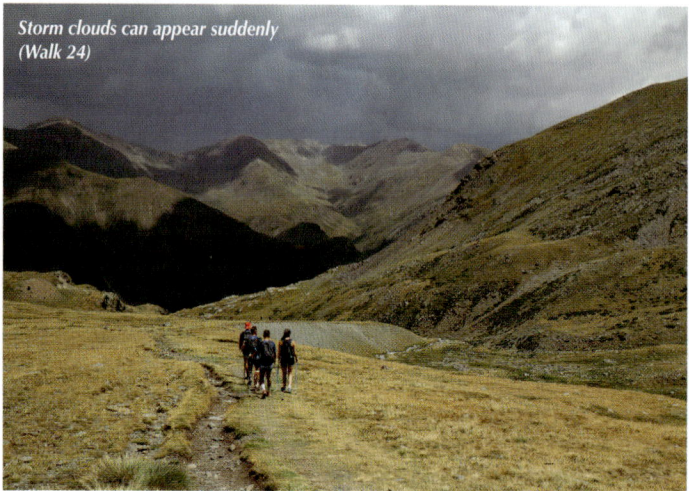

Storm clouds can appear suddenly (Walk 24)

Choose any trails in the Girona Pyrenees and without doubt your steps will be accompanied by far-reaching dramatic views. When the snow melts away, hikers replace the skiers, and fresh streams race down the grassy slopes where cattle graze and marmots look for food during the summer months. There are endless trails where the views are dominated by a sea of mountains as far as you can see.

From Queralbs follow the Camí Vell de Núria trail (Walk 23) or take the scenic rack railway to Núria and climb Puigmal (Walk 24) or Finestrelles (Walk 25). There is a hotel and also a campsite in Núria if you want to spend a few days exploring the mountains in this magical place.

You can also find accommodation in the quiet Queralbs or in the lively Ribes de Freser, where you can find everything a walker might need.

The cooler mountain temperatures in Setcases and Camprodon have always attracted people from the big cities, and both villages have some attractive summer houses. The cobbled streets are lined with restaurants and small shops where you can buy local products, such as honey, dried wild mushrooms, cheese or the traditional herbal liqueur ratafia. You can find hotels and restaurants that offer great local dishes, and there are also several campsites in the area.

There are regular trains from Barcelona to Ripoll and Ribes de Freser. Local buses can be used to access the smaller towns and villages.

WALK 14

Via Romana

Start	Sant Pau de Segúries, N42.261310, E2.365898
Distance	11km (there and back)
Total ascent/descent	600m
Grade	1
Time	4hr
Refreshments	Cafés, restaurants in Sant Pau de Segúries; Font de l'Arç spring at around 1.6km.
Access	Sant Pau de Segúries is located along the C-38 road, 6km south from Camprodon.
Public transport	Buses from Ripoll.

This well-signposted trail follows a road that is believed to have been built during Roman times as a branch of the Via Augusta. The exceptionally well-preserved road is dotted with the remains of some great feats of Roman engineering, such as drainage channels and some ruined buildings that served as hostels for travellers. The path was used until recently to drive cattle to the Pyrenean pastures for the summer months.

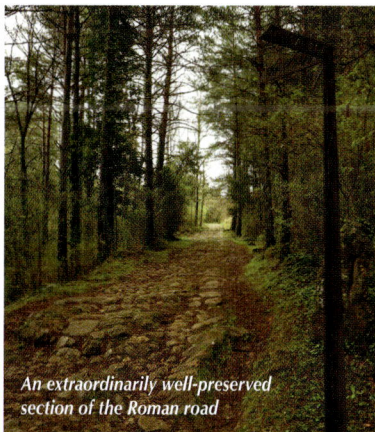

An extraordinarily well-preserved section of the Roman road

Follow Avenue El Mariner, passing Càmping Els Roures, and after the **campsite** at the junction with several waymarkers go right for Via Romana. Pass the **Sant Pau Vell Church**, cross the road and carry straight on passing the historic **Hostal de Dalt guest house**. Go past another tourist accommodation and shortly after leave the narrow tarmac road to the right by another house.

At the SP4 junction go left on Via Romana (Font de l'Arç spring is to the right). Ascend alongside a fence and at the next junction

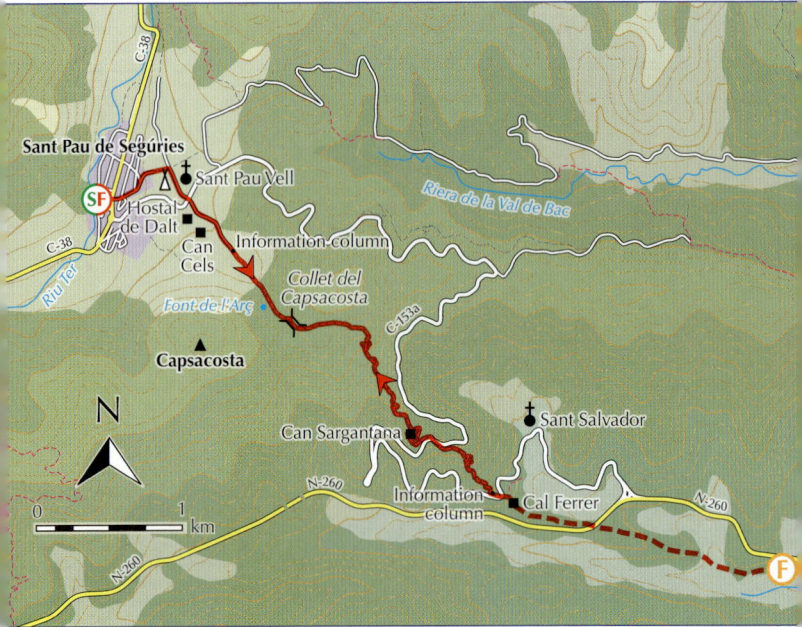

keep left. Soon reach **Collet del Capsacosta** with a small route information board. Ignore the narrow path on the left and descend on the wide cobbled path with some information signs towards the Bianya valley. There are some alternatives to the Via Romana; however, these always rejoin the main route. If you descend on the main route, you reach and cross the C-153 road about 1hr 30min from the Sant Pau Vell church, then you continue to descend the main route for a further 20min and reach the C-153 road again. During this descent there are also alternatives that divert and rejoin the main route. Cross the C-153 road and head to the ruins of **Cal Ferrer**. From the ruins retrace your steps to **Sant Pau de Segúries**.

Alternative to Pass de Traginers car park

Alternatively you can follow the Via Romana route for a further 3km to Pass de Traginers car park, which is located along the N-260 road where the signposted Via Romana starts and finishes. It is waymarked; however, there is less evidence of the Via Romana on this section. From the car park you have to arrange your transport or retrace your steps to **Sant Pau de Segúries**.

WALK 15

Camprodon to Sant Antoni

Start/finish	Camprodon, Parc Mare de la Font, N42.227432, E2.139612
Distance	5km
Total ascent/descent	420m
Grade	1
Time	2hr
Refreshments	Cafés and restaurants in Camprodon; spring at the start of the walk.
Access	Camprodon is located on the C-38 road 6km north of Sant Pau de Segúries. Coming from the south, just after the first roundabout, turn off for the Parc Mare de la Font car park.
Public transport	Buses from Ripoll.

From the shady picnic site at the edge of the charming Camprodon take the short but occasionally steep path to the 18th-century Ermita de Sant Antoni. The panoramic views are dominated by the high mountains of the Pyrenees and the ridge of the Serra Cavallera on the opposite side of the valley.

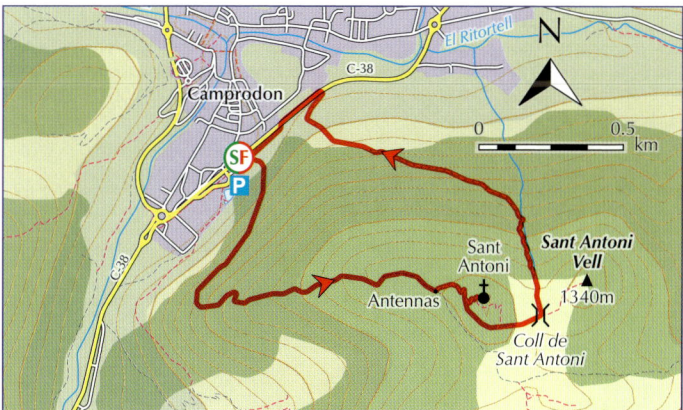

Facing the Mare de la Font spring, keep slightly right towards Sant Antoni on the path marked with yellow/white signs through beech forest. The path soon steepens and passes a possible entrance of a defence position from the Franco era. Ignoring the 'La Canal' route on the left, carry straight on. Follow the forest path on the mountainside and you soon have some views towards Camprodon. There is a short and steep section with some chains to help the climb. Nearing the top, reach a couple of **telecom antennas** and skirt by the fence, then continue on a track by the building. There are some unobstructed views to the north. Just before the track widens look out for and take the narrow path among trees on the left. Ascend for a few minutes and

The bell tower of the Sant Antoni church

Great views of Vall de Camprodon

Views of Camprodon on the steep ascent

climb some steps to reach the **Sant Antoni Church**. There are some picnic tables and great views towards the surrounding mountains. You can easily identify the magnificent ridge of the Serra Cavallera to the west across the valley. You can walk around the church building for further views.

From the church descend back to the first small junction (you came from the right) and take the path on the left downhill. Ignore the path on the left and then, shortly after on the right, follow the yellow/white marked path. When the path turns sharply right, take the path on the left steeply downhill and soon notice a yellow marker. Follow the grassy path curving downhill, passing a carved rock at **Coll de Sant Antoni**.

Follow the yellow signs downhill through forest for about 20–30min. Walk alongside the field and then cross it to reach the C-38 road. Turn left and follow the road, then shortly after take the path on the left side of the road that leads back to Mare de la Font.

After your walk you may want to spend some time wandering the cobbled streets of **Camprodon** built on the banks of the River Ter. Cross the picturesque medieval stone bridge and sample some local dishes in the restaurants.

WALK 16

Serra Cavallera ridge from Camprodon

Start/finish	Camprodon car and campervan car park, N42.312057, E2.363093
Distance	18.5km
Total ascent/descent	1030m
Grade	3
Time	6hr 30min–7hr
Refreshments	Cafés, restaurants in Camprodon; none along the way.
Access	Camprodon is located 6km north of Sant Pau de Segúries on the C-38 road. In Camprodon take the GIV-5264 road and then go left and follow Carrer de Joan Manén for 250 metres to a circular car park for cars and campervans.
Public transport	Buses from Ripoll.

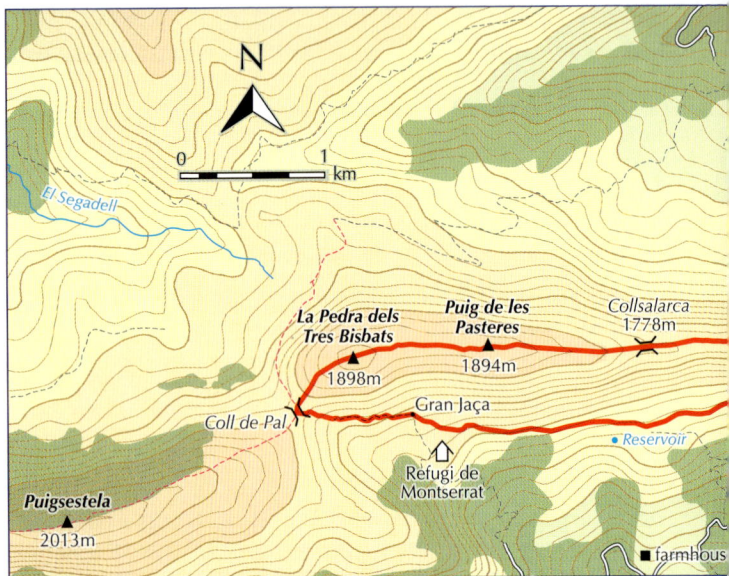

This long, spectacular route climbs and follows the ridge of the Serra Cavallera mountain range. The massif lies between the Ter and Freser river valleys, and from the peaks that reach up to around 2000m you can enjoy splendid views to the higher mountains of the Pyrenees. From La Pedra dels Tres Bisbats – the highest point on the route – the descent to the south is equally rewarding. Traversing the meadows to Pla d'en Plata can be a little challenging due to some route-finding difficulties.

From the car park follow the yellow signs on Carrer de Joan Manén and leave the road to the right on a path in the road bend. Ascend initially alongside a drystone retaining wall and through forest. Follow the yellow/white signs ignoring any unmarked paths. Reach a junction with a sign with faint writing on it (**Les Marrades**). Go right uphill (you will return to this junction from the left). Ascend through forest and when you reach a wider path at **Coll d'en Gener** continue straight on uphill, ignoring a path on the left marked with yellow signs. This is a steep climb on a narrow path with occasional views of the mountains. You can spot Sant Antoni church perched on the nearby mountain above Camprodon.

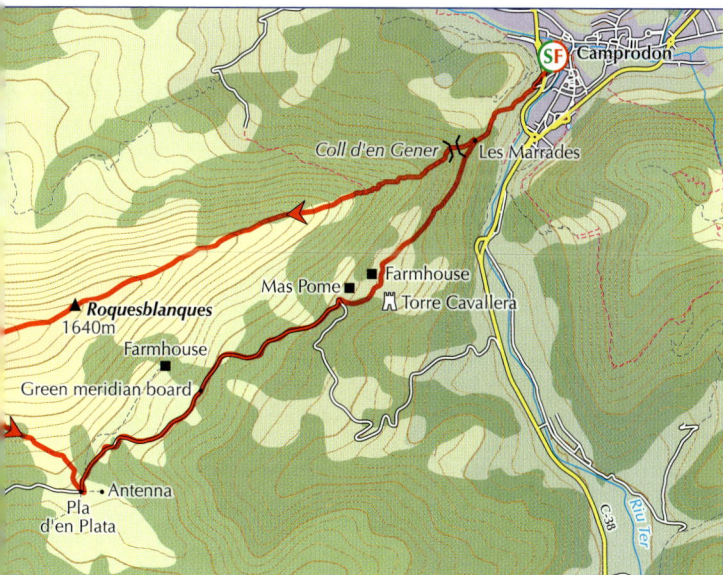

79

Ignore the path marked with cairns (this drops down to Llanars) and climb the ridge. Follow the path, often alongside a wire fence, and soon pass the first of the several large cairns dotted on the ridge. On your right the views are dominated by the higher mountains of the Pyrenees. On a clear day it is also possible to make out the mountains of the Montseny and Montserrat ranges in the distance to the south and on the left. Just over 3hr after starting the climb from Camprodon, at 7km, reach **Puig de les Pasteres** (alt. 1894m). Then 15–20min later, at 8km, reach **La Pedra dels Tres Bisbats** (alt. 1898m), where an extensive panorama greets you.

From the summit follow the yellow/white signs down to **Coll de Pal** and keep left towards Camprodon (marked 3hr 15m away). Descend on the grassy mountainside, which is used for grazing, passing a trough. The ridge that you

The weather can change quickly up on the ridge, take some extra layers

The route is easy to follow on the ridge

traversed is above on the left. At Gran Jaça, R49 junction with signpost, keep left and look out for yellow signs on rocks. From here you can see the building of the **Refugi de Montserrat** on the right, lower down on the mountainside. The meadow is scattered with rocks that are occasionally marked with yellow signs. There are a few farm houses dotted around on the lower slopes. There is a network of paths made and used by cattle, and if you lose the signs head in the direction of the tall antennas in the near distance at Pla d'en Plata. As you get closer to this junction try to keep closer to the treeline. Descend to a sealed road – **Pla d'en Plata** – and keep left towards Camprodon. There are some yellow signs along the road. Follow the tarmac road for about 25–30min ignoring a track to Can Fancó on the left. About 1km later leave the tarmac road to the left towards Camprodon and El Puixeu, and after a few metres go through an iron gate. The remains of the medieval tower, **Torre Cavallera**, is on your right as you follow the track downhill. Overlooking the Ter river valley, Torre Cavallera was most probably a watch tower, and was used as a signal tower.

Pass some stone buildings and reach El Puixen, R68 junction. Keep right towards Camprodon and walk alongside pastures. Shortly after, descend through forest and reach **Les Marrades** junction (you went up on the path now on the left). Continue straight on downhill back to **Camprodon**.

WALK 17
Camí de Carboneres

Start/finish	Village car park located on the GIV-5264 road in Setcases, N42.375692, E2.302606
Distance	11.5km
Total ascent/descent	750m
Grade	2
Time	4hr 30min
Refreshments	Cafés/restaurants in Setcases; none along the way.
Access	Setcases is located on the GIV-5264 road 12km north of Camprodon – parking is available by the main road near the bridge.
Public transport	Buses from Ripoll.

The trail described mainly follows the signposted Carboneres trail with an extension to Refugi Jaume Ferrer. Climb alongside the Carboner river, passing some wonderful waterfalls with glorious views to the nearby mountains. Allow some time to stroll the narrow streets of the charming Setcases, which attracts visitors with traditional local products.

Follow the GIV-5264 road alongside the River Ter, passing the bridge in the village (you will return to Setcases via this bridge). Leaving the houses of Setcases, the road crosses the river just after passing **Font del Pont Nou**. Entering the Parc Natural de les Capçaleres del Ter i el Freser, follow the tarmac road towards the towering mountains. When you have walked 1.7km from the car park, leave the tarmac road to join the Camí de Carboneres trail on the right by the signpost near a house.

Ascend with the Carboner river on your left for about 200 metres and pass a sign that marks a narrow path climbing to **Balma de les Donzelles**, a natural rock shelter. Follow the yellow signs uphill alongside the rushing river. Shortly pass a wooden sign that marks a narrow, steep path on the right leading to **Mare de Déu dels Àngels del Carboners**, a shrine higher up the mountainside.

The path marked with yellow signs continues to climb by the river. Cross the river on a bridge, and shortly after pass the **Salt del Cossi d'en Batlló waterfall**. Cross the river on rocks twice and then cross a **footbridge**. The water is rushing

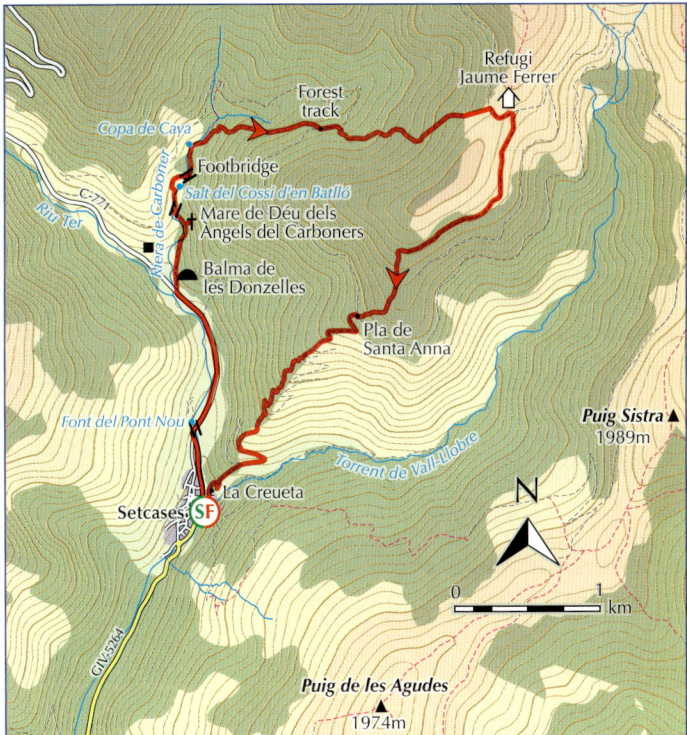

down on rocks near the path as you ascend. For about 30min, climb the path marked with the yellow signs through forest with occasional views to the towering mountains nearby, ignoring any unmarked paths and paths marked with blue markers before reaching a forest track. Keep left on the track towards Refugi Jaume Ferrer (the signposted Carboneres trail continues to the right). Follow the track for about 150 metres and, just before reaching an information board, go right on a narrow path towards Refugi Jaume Ferrer. Ascend through forest on the path marked with orange signs for about 10–15min and reach an open meadow where great mountain views greet you. Follow the orange signs painted on rocks uphill by the treeline.

Walk through forest again before emerging on to another meadow. Look out for the orange signs on rocks as you ascend with amazing mountain views.

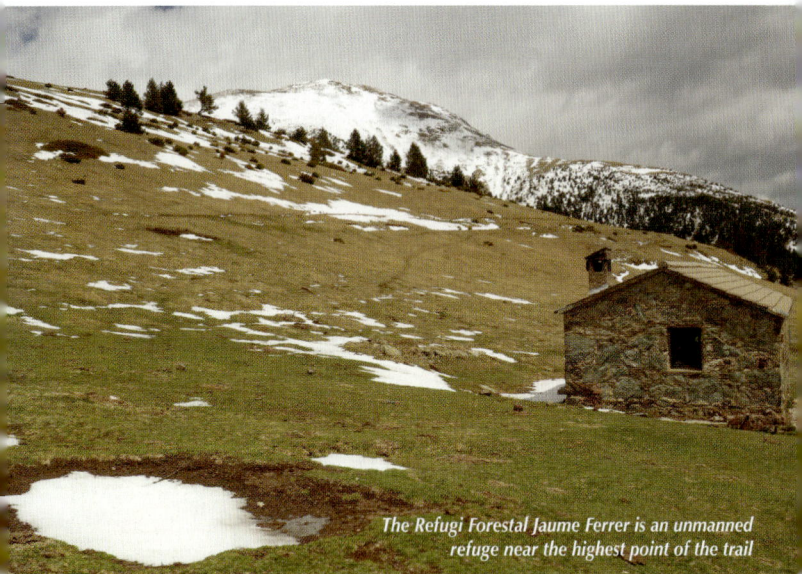

The Refugi Forestal Jaume Ferrer is an unmanned refuge near the highest point of the trail

Meet a track and go right, and a few minutes later arrive at **Refugi Jaume Ferrer** (alt. 1977m).

With the entrance of the refuge behind you, look out for a blue paintmark by the trough. Keeping the trough on your right, descend on a path with some great views. Leave this path to the left marked with a blue marker (ignore the wider path that continues straight, marked with a blue 'X'). Descend on the narrow path through pine forest, cross a meadow and then continue through the pine forest for about 20min to reach a forest track at **Pla de Santa Anna**. Cross over and continue on its other side, slightly to the right by the map board. There you rejoin the Carboneres route and the path is marked with yellow signs again. Follow the yellow signs downhill, ignoring any other paths for about an hour. Descend initially on the wide path with some excellent views to the nearby mountains, including the impressive Gra de Fajol towering over the Ter river valley. When the path splits near the wire fence, keep right on the yellow marked path and zigzag downhill through pine forest with more and more views towards Setcases. Pass a building and head towards the village with the river Torrent de Vall-Llobre below on the left. Pass the viewpoint with a cross, **La Creueta**, just above the village, and shortly after arrive back at the bridge and spring in **Setcases**.

Great views of Gra de Fajol, one of the mountains overlooking the Ter river valley

WALK 18
Gra de Fajol

Start/finish	Parking area near Vall de Ter, N42.400445, E2.278235
Distance	12.5km
Total ascent/descent	1110m
Grade	3
Time	5hr 30min–6hr
Refreshments	None along the way, but there is a café at Refugi d'Ulldeter slightly off the route.
Access	From Setcases continue on the C-771 road for about 6km towards Vallter 2000; there are parking places just off the road.
Public transport	Buses from Ripoll and Camprodon to Setcases.

The route initially follows the River Ter upriver and then takes you above the popular ski slopes of Vallter 2000 to the summit of Gra de Fajol. A sea of mighty mountains dominates the landscape as far as you can see. This route is best in the spring after the snow melts away or in the summer when the temperatures stay in the early twenties. During the descent look out for marmots and Pyrenean chamois.

From the C-771 road take the GR11 trail marked with red/white stripes uphill. A few minutes later the path splits; go right on the GR11 trail (you will return to this junction from the path on the left). Climb the wide path lined with electricity poles alongside the River Ter. Cross the river on rocks and pass the spring, Font del Sauc. About 45min–1hr from the start reach a tarmac road near the lowest car park of Vallter 2000. Keep left on the road, passing a car park, and then walk across the next car park heading towards the ski lifts. Pass the ticket office and go under the **ski lift**. Start on the blue slope steeply uphill and soon you can spot the other car parks and further ski lifts on the mountainside. Towering mountains dominate the landscape.

The path levels on a grassy area, and then climbs again towards the towering Gra de Fajol. Soon the refuge building comes into view. Ignore a path with cairns on the left and stay on the wide path that heads towards and then skirts beneath

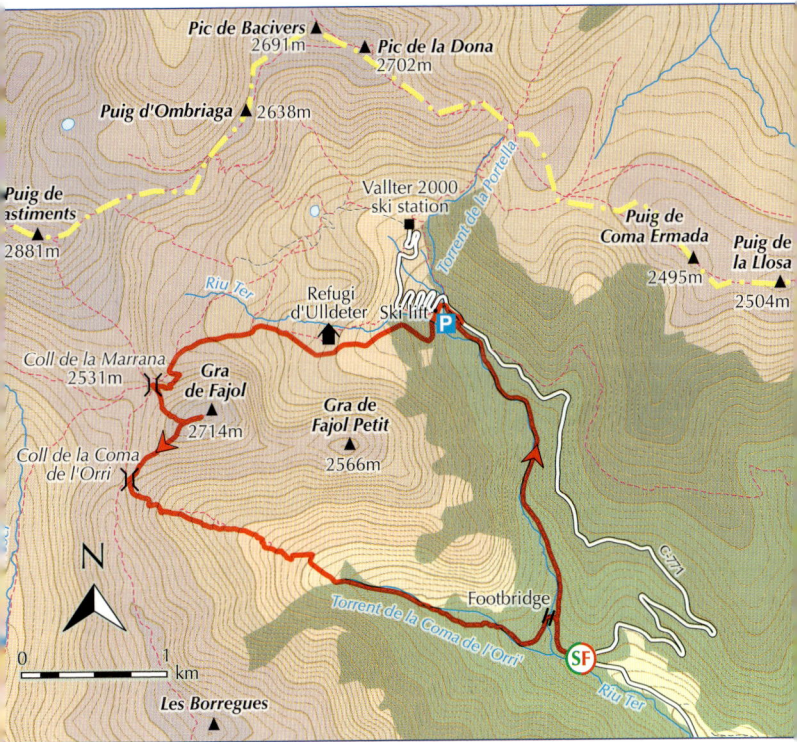

the refuge building with towering mountains on your left. Notice a path joining from the right from the refuge (**Refugi d'Ulldeter**), but continue on the 'blue' ski slope. Shortly after, you rejoin the GR11 route and follow the red/white signs uphill. At a junction with a signpost go left uphill towards Coll de la Marrana on the GR11 path. (Another path goes right to the source of the River Ter.) Cross a ski slope and continue straight on uphill with the rugged mountain of Gra de Fajol on your left.

At the junction with a signpost go left towards Coll de la Marrana. Ignore the path marked with an 'X' on the right and zigzag uphill on the well-trodden path to **Coll de la Marrana** where, at the big path junction, you go left uphill. There are no signs, but cairns mark the well-trodden path all the way to the top. Keep left when you reach the ridge (you will return to this point from the summit). Climb to the summit of **Gra de Fajol** (alt. 2714m) and enjoy the 360-degree panorama. The immediate views are dominated by the nearby Gra de Fajol Petit, Pic de la Dona and Bastiments. As far as you can see, mountains fill the horizon, and below you can see the ski slopes of Vallter 2000.

Peak of Bastiments viewed from Col de la Marrana

Gra de Fajol is one of the most popular mountaintops around Vallter 2000

From the peak descend back on the ridge and, when the path bends right downhill, continue straight on the ridge and then descend towards the col. Shortly you will notice some stone cairns marking the very faint path. About 20–30min from the peak reach the pile of rocks at **Coll de la Coma de l'Orri** and keep diagonally left to locate the next stone cairn. Follow the cairns downhill, initially on the grassy mountainside that is used for grazing cattle, with Gra de Fajol Petit and the ridge dominating the scenery.

Occasionally you have to cross narrow streams racing down on the slope and then walk among pine trees. Emerging from the trees, keep right on the meadow, and shortly after get close to and then cross a stream. There are some painted blue signs as you descend among pines. The aftermath of a huge landslide can be seen on the nearby mountainside.

Cross the stream on rocks then keep right downhill. Reach a wider path and go left, then follow the cairns leaving the wide path to the left. Cross the stream on rocks again. After descending for nearly two hours from Coll de la Coma de l'Orri cross the wooden **footbridge** over the River Ter and reach the junction with a signpost you passed near the start of the walk. Keep right and soon arrive back at the starting point.

WALK 19

Pic de la Dona and Bastiments

Start/finish	Vallter 2000 top car park, N42.426808, E2.265483
Distance	12km
Total ascent/descent	900m
Grade	3
Time	4hr 30min–5hr
Refreshments	Café at Refugi d'Ulldeter, snack bar at Vallter 2000.
Access	The large car park of Vallter 2000 is located at the very end of C-771, about 12km north of Setcases.
Public transport	Buses from Olot and Camprodon.

The route described takes in Pic de la Dona as well as Pic de Bastiments. Both mountains are located along the breathtaking ridge on the Spanish–French border. This walk is best in the late spring, once the snow melts away, or on a clear summer day when magnificent mountains fill the horizon as far as you can see. From the summit of Bastiments the trail drops down to Coll de la Marrana and then visits the source of the River Ter before returning to Vallter 2000 ski station.

Locate the wooden signpost near the snack bar and keep slightly right towards Pic de la Dona, following the path behind the main building. The path leads up and away from the ski station and car park. A few minutes after the start, at the path junction, go left uphill on the GR76 trail. Follow the red/white signs uphill for about 15min (ignoring paths marked with a red/white 'X') and reach the ridge at the **Portella de Mentet** (alt. 2415m) signpost on the French border. Keep left uphill on the ridge and climb the most prominent, often rocky, path with views towards Gra de Fajol on the opposite side of the valley. After about 30min reach the summit of **Pic de la Dona** (alt. 2702m) where you are greeted with a 360-degree panorama. There are spectacular views of the ridge, which forms a natural border with France, and of the ski slopes below on the mountainside, and on a clear day you can see all the way to the Montseny Massif.

From the peak continue on the path downhill and notice some border markers on the ridge – the path often runs on the Spanish–French border. Ignore a faint

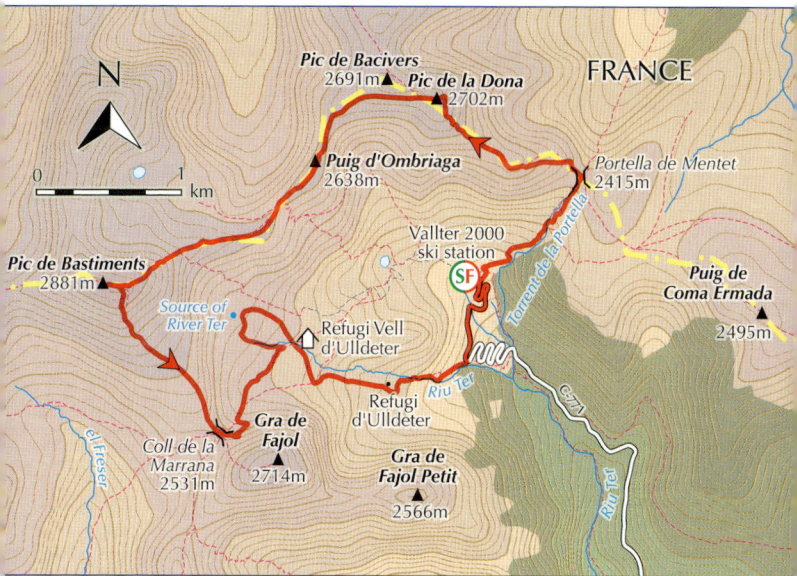

Battered flag on top of Pic de la Dona (2702m)

The peaks of Gra de Fajol (2714m) and Bastiments (2881m) overshadowing the valley

path that drops down towards the ski slopes on the left. When the path bends sharply right down towards the valley on the French side, carry straight on, initially close to the other path, and follow the rock cairns on the narrow ridge line through the barren landscape towards the towering Bastiments in front of you. Shortly after you start the steep ascent.

Ignore another path dropping steeply down towards the ski slopes on the left and continue to climb. Make your way to the cross and then on to the cairn marking the top of **Pic de Bastiments** (alt. 2881m). Reach the summit about 1hr 30min from Pic de la Dona. There are sweeping views of the Pyrenees and on a clear day you can make out the Montserrat and Montseny mountain ranges in the distance.

From the peak go back to the cross and then take the path steeply downhill slightly to the right in the direction of Gra de Fajol. With the cross behind you, zigzag downhill towards the col. Descend for about 30min and arrive at **Coll de la Marrana**, and go left downhill on the GR11 path marked with red/white signs.

A few minutes later, at the next junction with a signpost, go left towards the Refugi vell d'Ulldeter. It is marked with a red/white 'X'; however, there are some yellow signs to follow. You are now walking just below Pic de Bastiments. Shortly before reaching a ski slope turn left uphill by the trickling River Ter on the path marked with red/white signs to climb to the **source of the River Ter** (Naixement del Ter) at the altitude of 2480m.

> The **Capçaleres del Ter i del Freser Natural Park** was created in 2015 and covers an area of 14,500 hectares in the high Ripollès region. Its mountains reach close to 3000m. As the name suggests, the park is home to two important rivers, the Ter and the Freser, and their sources.

From the source go right downhill on the ski slope and follow it for about 600 metres, and then take the path on the left towards Refugi d'Ulldeter (0.4km away) and Carratera-aparcament (1.1km away). Before taking the path to the refuge you can make a short detour by following the signposted path to the ruins of the **Refugi Vell d'Ulldeter** (old refuge) that is located near the ski slope to the left. Follow the path passing the **Refugi d'Ulldeter** all the way to the road; keep left on the tarmac road and follow it back to the large car park at **Vallter 2000**.

CÈSAR AUGUST TORRAS I FERRERI

Cèsar August Torras i Ferreri, a mountaineer (and a broker by trade), is believed to have been the first promoter of Catalan hiking. He was very fond of the area and he even published several hiker's guides in the early 20th century (*Guia itinerari de l'excursionista a Camprodon*, 1902). He wanted to create a network of mountain refuges. Refugi vell d'Ulldeter – built in a noucentista style – was one of the first mountain refuges built in Catalunya. Its location was chosen because of its close proximity to the source of the River Ter and because it could provide easy access to the nearby high mountains. It opened in July 1909 and was operating until the civil war, when it was partially demolished by the Francoists to prevent the Maquis sheltering there.

WALK 20

Seven gorges trail

Start/finish	Campdevànol, Àrea Lleure de Font del Querol, N42.227502, E2.139531
Distance	9km
Total ascent/descent	250m
Grade	1
Time	2hr 30min–3hr
Refreshments	Kiosk near the last waterfall and shop at Camping Pirinenc.
Access	The car park is next to Camping Pirinenc, located 2.5km west of Campdevànol along the GI-401 road. There is a ticket booth here. To control the number of visitors in the gorge, there is a €5 entrance fee between 10 June and 30 September. If you are staying at the Camping Pirinenc located next to the trail head, you can get a €3 discount.
Public transport	Buses from Ripoll to Campdevànol.

This popular, well-signposted trail takes you to a series of rock pools with waterfalls. It is considered one of the must-visit attractions in the area and – because of its easy terrain and accessibility – the route can get busy, especially on warm, sunny days.

The trail starts from Àrea de Lleure de la Font del Querol, a picnic site and car park with a kiosk where you can buy tickets to access the trail in the summer months. Go through the barrier and walk alongside the river. At the T-junction keep left alongside pastures, shortly passing the entrance of an adventure park and its car park. Reach a **ticket booth** where your ticket will be checked, then continue on the sealed forest track. Ignore another track on the right and soon leave the track to the left downhill through forest at the start of the 'Els 7 Gorgs' trail, marked with a wooden sign.

Shortly after, come to the path that leads down to **Gorg de la Cabana**, the first of the seven waterfalls. The path to the waterfall can be slippery and muddy in places. From the waterfall climb back to the main path and continue towards

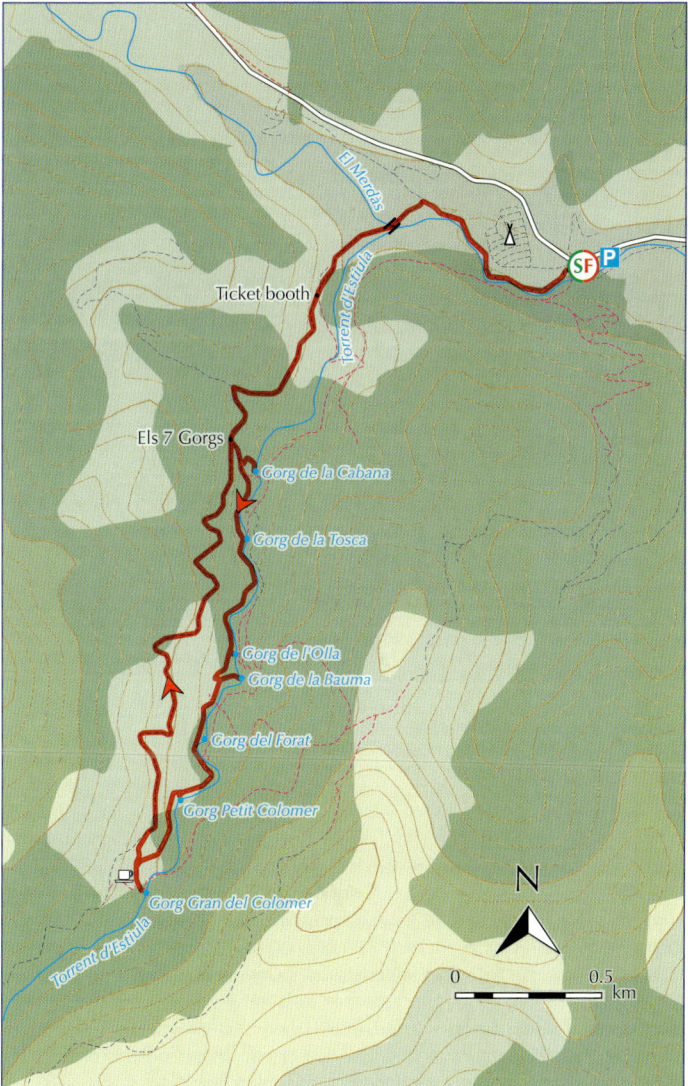

El Merdàs

SF P

Ticket booth

Torrent d'Estula

Els 7 Gorgs

Gorg de la Cabana

Gorg de la Tosca

Gorg de l'Olla
Gorg de la Bauma

Gorg del Forat

Gorg Petit Colomer

Gorg Gran del Colomer

Torrent d'Estula

N

0   0.5
            km

The Gorg de l'Olla is the smallest of the seven small waterfalls

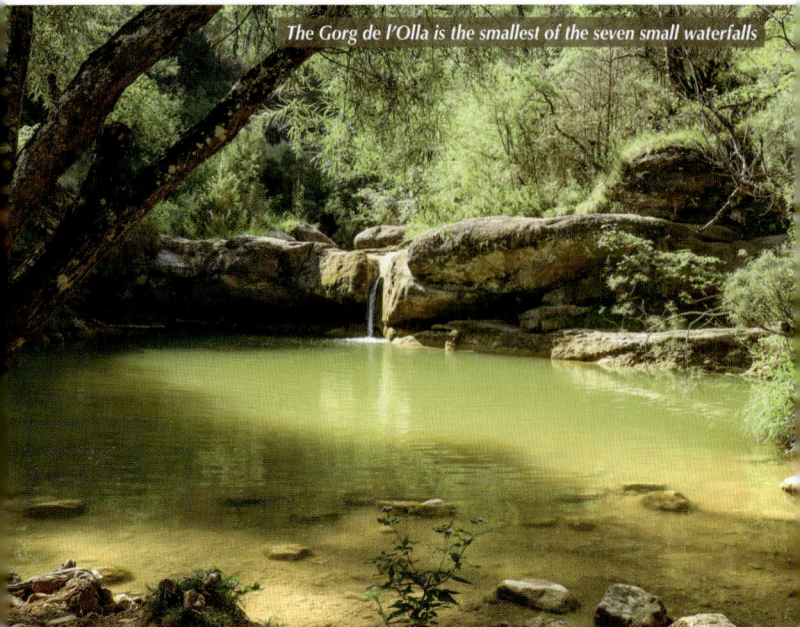

the second waterfall, Gorg de la Tosca. There are some other paths but the route to the rock pools is well trodden and well signposted. Walk through forest and alongside the river. From the main path walk to **Gorg de la Tosca**, which is not far away, and then to the third waterfall, **Gorg de l'Olla**. Return to the junction and continue along the path.

Reach a junction and go left following the signs towards 'Gorgs 4, 5, 6, 7'. When the path splits, go left and descend to **Gorg de la Bauma**. Return to the main path and continue towards 'Gorg 5'. Cross another path and carry straight on along the well-trodden path to **Gorg del Forat**. Return to the junction and continue alongside the river to the sixth waterfall, **Gorg Petit Colomer**. Carry on following the yellow markers, keep left and soon pass a kiosk with refreshments, then go left downhill to the last waterfall, **Gorg Gran del Colomer**.

From the last waterfall return to the kiosk and then take the track marked 'Pista Forestal'. Reach a track and go right, then follow it with some views for about 20min to the point where the 'Els 7 Gorgs' trail starts. Continue on the track and retrace your steps to the **car park**, which is about 30min away.

WALK 21
Taga from Ribes de Freser

Start/finish	Ribes-Vila rack railway station in Ribes de Freser, N42.308711, E2.171522
Distance	13km (there and back)
Total ascent/descent	1170m
Grade	3
Time	5hr
Refreshments	Cafés and restaurants in Ribes de Freser; none along the way.
Access	Ribes de Freser is located on the N-260 road 14km north from Ripoll.
Public transport	Trains from Ripoll.

This is a steep, demanding climb to the 2040m-high Taga, the highest peak of the Serra Cavallera mountain range. From Ribes de Freser the signposted trail initially follows tracks and then climbs the demanding steep, grassy mountainside. Your efforts will be generously rewarded with a fantastic panorama towards the higher mountains in the Pyreenes.

Facing the Ribes-Vila rack railway station go left on Plaça de l'Estació road, crossing the railway. The road becomes a track and bends right up by an information board. At Sota Font de la Margarideta, RF14 junction, carry straight on on the broad path that runs just above the village, passing Font de la Margarideta (spring). A few minutes later at Font de Sta Caterina (spring) go left uphill on the Ribes de Freser–Taga trail.

Ascend the well-trodden path marked with yellow signs through forest. At a track junction continue straight on uphill. Soon leave the track to the left for a short while before rejoining it again and going left. Shortly after, leave the track again to the right uphill on a path. On your left are the first views of the mountains. Emerge from the forest and keep right by a field. At the track junction with signpost, take the second track from the right uphill towards Cim de Taga. Follow the track that winds uphill with some views, and then spot a well-preserved **pillbox** from the Franco era.

This now overgrown bunker/pillbox was part of Franco's Pyrenees defence line

Climb steadily, first through forest and then on the grassy hillside. Follow the yellow signs alongside pasture land with far-reaching views on your right. Stay on the track and arrive at **Plans de Conivella**, RF6 junction, about 40–45min after joining the track. Continue straight uphill towards Cim del Taga (note the time, 1hr 40min to the summit, which suggests a demanding ascent!). Climb steeply and constantly along a low wire fence with views towards the surrounding mountains and soon pass a viewpoint board which (curiously) marks the mountains visible from the summit, though this is still far away. However, the views are great and you can admire the higher mountains around Vall de Núria to the north.

Continue the steep climb among trees for a short while, and before long you are on the grassy mountainside again. Shortly before starting the final ascent, reach a fence, then carry on climbing alongside it and arrive at the summit of **Taga** (alt. 2040m) about 3hr from Ribes de Freser. From the top, the spectacular ridge of Serra Cavallera unfolds and to the north there are views of the high mountains that hug Vall de Núria. Return to **Ribes de Freser** the same way you came.

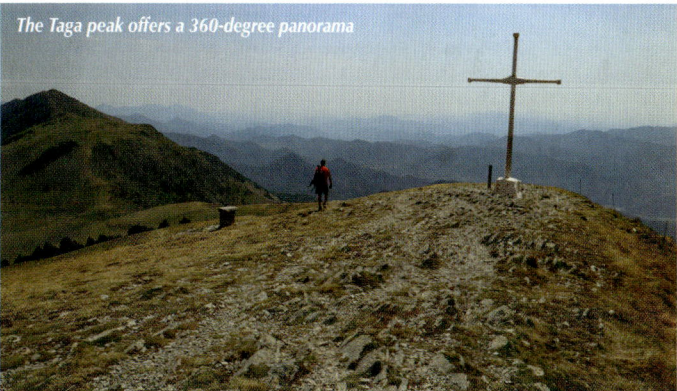

The Taga peak offers a 360-degree panorama

WALK 22
Queralbs to Font de l'Home Mort

Start/finish	Queralbs rack railway station, N42.351299, E2.165676
Distance	14.5km
Total ascent/descent	940m
Grade	2
Time	5hr–5hr 30min
Refreshments	Café and restaurant in Queralbs; none along the way.
Access	There is a large car park by the rack railway station at the edge of Queralbs, which is located on the GIV-5217 road, about 8km north of Ribes de Freser.
Public transport	Rack railway from Ribes de Freser.

This delightful route allows you to enjoy some nice mountain views without a demanding climb. The first part of the route follows a well-signposted section of the GR11 trail to the Font de l'Home Mort spring tucked away in the valley and surrounded by spectacular mountains. It is a fairly easy trail; however, there is a short but very steep downhill section before reaching Mina Zaragoza.

From the station walk to the centre of Queralbs village. At the square with the fountain go left on the GR11 trail (to the right, the GR11 climbs to Núria). Follow the red/white signs among traditional stone houses to **Església de Sant Jaume**. Go right uphill by the church, then keep sharply left. There are red/white and yellow signs to follow.

Shortly after, leave the road to the right uphill on a path that initially runs parallel to the road above a house. Soon cross a driveway by **Ermita de Sant Sebastià** and continue straight on by a cultivated patch of land. A few minutes later cross a track by Sota de la Cabanya del Pintor, R221 signpost, and continue on the slightly overgrown GR11 trail straight on. When you reach a track again, keep left with some mountain views.

At the next junction follow the red/white signs straight on, crossing the river on a bridge, and then leave the track to the right at **Prat del Barló**, Q1 junction, towards Font de l'Home Mort. As you ascend among trees, notice a retaining

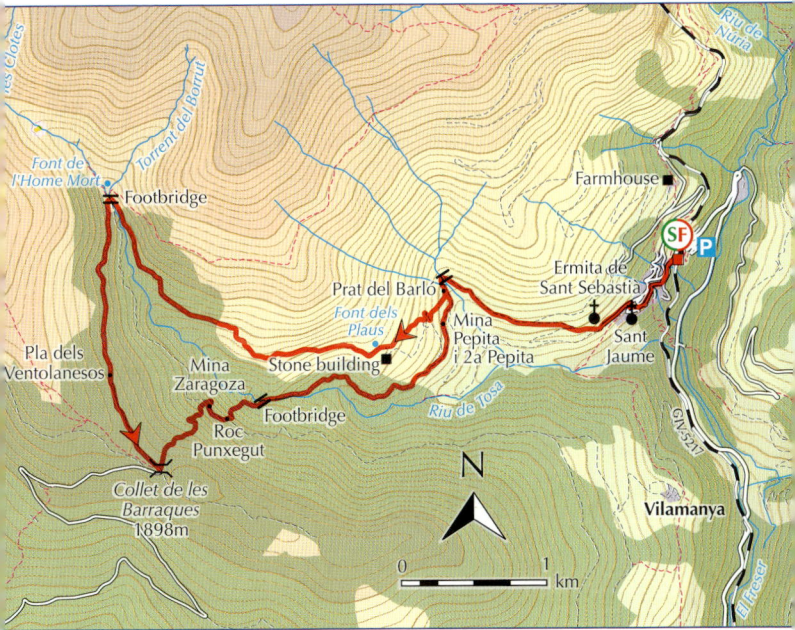

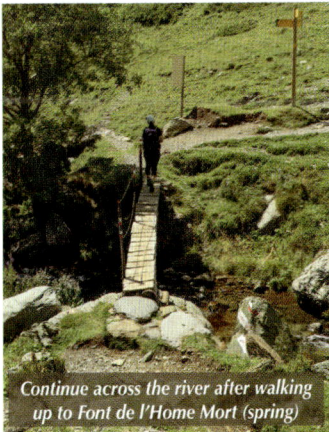
Continue across the river after walking up to Font de l'Home Mort (spring)

wall. Reach a track, go right and a few minutes later leave the track to the right on a path marked with red/white signs. Ascend for about 10min and then pass a stone building and the nearby **Font dels Plaus spring**. The views are dominated by the towering mountains on your right and the gorge of the River Tosa on the left. Follow the signs initially uphill among shrubs and trees. Pass a small stone shepherd's hut on the way and, about 1hr from the Font dels Plaus spring, reach a **footbridge** across the River Tosa. The spring – **Font de l'Home Mort** – is located a few metres up the path to the right.

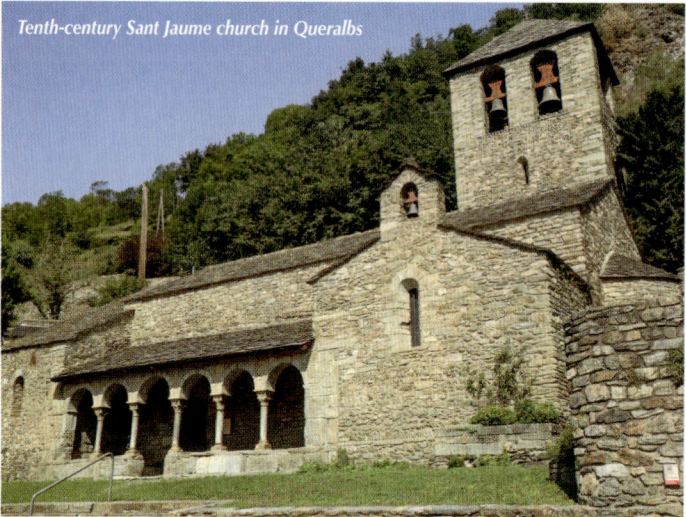
Tenth-century Sant Jaume church in Queralbs

Cross the footbridge and then at the Font de l'Home Mort Q2 junction take the path on the left uphill towards Queralbs (in the direction of Mina Saragossa/ Vilamanya) climbing above the track. Follow the GR11 through pine forest with occasional views to the mountains on the other side of the gorge. At a clearing, head to the **Pla dels Ventolanesos**, R198 signpost, and then keep left on the GR11 towards Queralbs. Follow the forest track on the pine tree-dotted hillside to **Collet de les Barraques** and turn sharply left just before the cattle grid. (There are picnic benches and a viewpoint at this col.) From there, follow the yellow signs. Descend steeply and turn sharply left downhill by the rock wall. There is a wire fence that you might have to step over. After a very steep descent, arrive on a track and go right with the deep gorge on your left. Follow the track downhill passing the entrance of **Mina Zaragoza** and reach **Roc Punxegut**, Q3 junction. Leave the track to the left towards Queralbs. Following the yellow signs, zigzag downhill for about 15min to the bottom of the gorge and cross the River Tosa on a **footbridge**. Walk alongside a rock wall with the stream on your right; the path that follows the contour of the mountain soon becomes a track. Forested mountainsides dominate the scenery across the gorge. Reach a track in a bend and keep right. Pass a sign for another mine entrance, **Mina Pepita i 2a Pepita**. Ignore a track on the right and arrive back at **Prat del Barló**, Q1 junction. Continue on the track and retrace your steps to the village (it is about 30min to the station).

WALK 23
Camí Vell de Núria

Start	Queralbs rack railway station, N42.351299, E2.165676
Finish	Vall de Núria
Distance	8km
Total ascent/descent	1050m/265m
Grade	2
Time	3hr
Refreshments	Café, restaurant and shop in both Queralbs and Núria.
Access	Queralbs is located on the GIV-5217 road, 8km north of Ribes de Freser – there is a large car park located near the train station at the edge of Queralbs.
Public transport	Train from Ribes de Freser.

Núria can only be accessed by the scenic rack railway or on foot. The most rewarding way to get to this stunning place is to follow the GR11 long-distance trail on the Camí Vell de Núria, the old path from Queralbs. It is a straightforward ascent to Núria with stunning views and waterfalls to admire. It is easy to spend a full day in Núria, and if you want to take the scenic railway back to Queralbs, it is advisable that you pre-book your tickets: www.valldenuria.cat.

From the station take the Camí Vell signposted trail to the village centre. At the small square with a fountain go right by the Queralbs-Plaça de Raig, R114 signpost. Follow the Camí Vell de Núria path that shares the route with the GR11 long-distance trail. Climb some steps and keep right then left uphill among the houses. Follow the red/white signs to the left and the paved road soon becomes a path. Reach and cross a road diagonally to the right and continue uphill towards Núria. Pass two more houses and soon the rack railway comes into view. Pass Font de la Ruïra, and then cross a small stream. On the old route to Núria it was customary to stop by the spring and drink its water with aniseed. At Tartera de Corbell junction continue straight on, crossing the scree towards Núria (pel pont de Cremal/GR11). About 10min later at Escales de Corbell junction carry straight on towards Núria (pel pont de Cremal). This section of the rocky path is a little more exposed and you have great views down to the river.

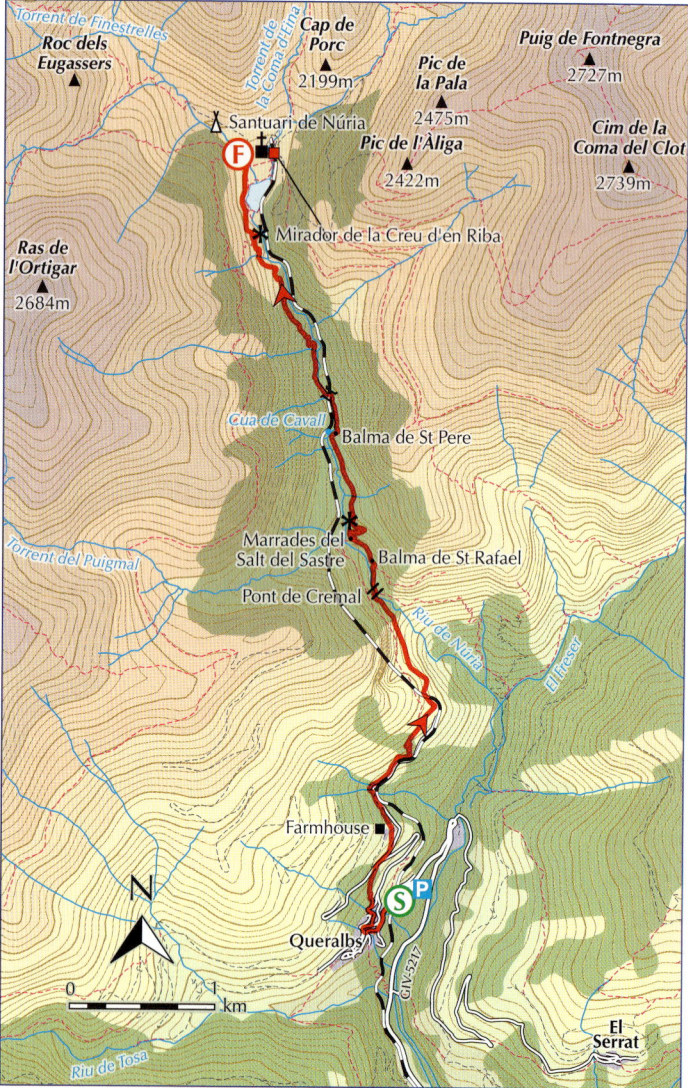

Roc dels
Eugassers

Torrent de Finestrelles

Torrent de
la Coma d'Eina

Cap de
Porc
2199m

Pic de
la Pala
2475m

Puig de Fontnegra
2727m

Santuari de Núria

F

Pic de l'Àliga
2422m

Cim de la
Coma del Clot
2739m

Mirador de la Creu d'en Riba

Ras de
l'Ortigar
2684m

Cua de Cavall

Balma de St Pere

Marrades del
Salt del Sastre

Balma de St Rafael

Pont de Cremal

Riu de Núria

El Freser

N

Farmhouse

S **P**

Queralbs

GIV-5217

0   1
km

Riu de Tosa

El
Serrat

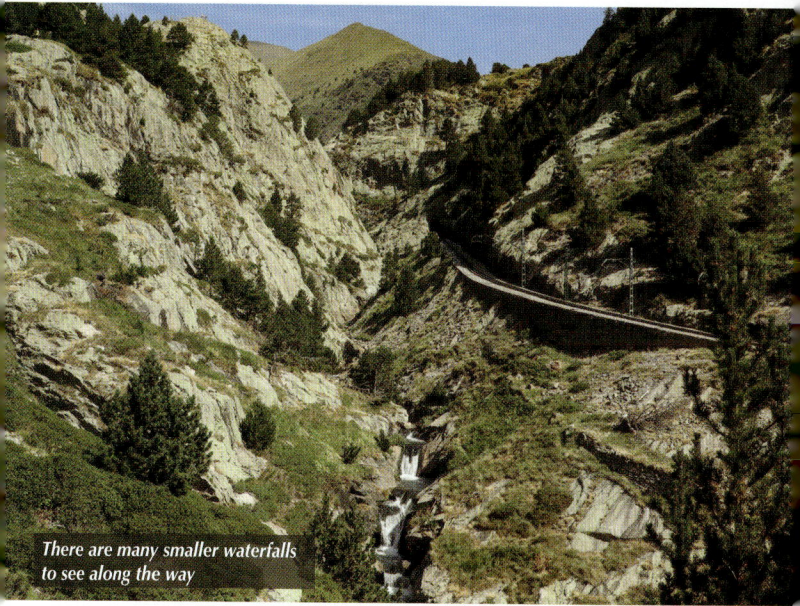

There are many smaller waterfalls to see along the way

Cross the stone bridge, **Pont de Cremal**, less than an hour from the tarmac road. Keep left uphill with the river gorge on your left, passing a natural rock shelter, **Balma de St Rafael**. Reach **Marrades del Salt del Sastre junction** and continue straight on. Zigzag uphill on the rocky mountainside with excellent views to the gorge. Soon reach a viewpoint, (Salt del Sastre), which provides a perfect vantage point to see the impressive Salt del Sastre waterfall across the gorge. Walk among pines and then on the more exposed mountainside; occasionally the rack railway comes into view as you ascend towards the towering mountains.

Pass Cua de Cavall waterfall on your left and shortly after pass another natural rock shelter, **Balma de St Pere**. Continue the ascent with constant views to the rushing river down below. The path passes under the railway and at the same time over the River Núria on a bridge. Climb with the river on your right and you can see the rack railway line across the valley.

Pass a marker for Torrent de la Coma de les Perdius (stream) and then climb some steps and reach a junction with signpost, Creu d'en Riba. Walk up to **Mirador de la Creu d'en Riba** on the right. Enjoy the views towards the lake and the buildings of Núria from the viewpoint. From the Creu d'en Riba junction

Vall de Núria viewed from Creu d'en Riba

continue on downhill passing the Hermitage of St Giles just before reaching **Santuari de Núria** (alt. 1958m).

ST GILES

According to legend, around 700AD, St Giles spent four years in the valley living in a cave and sharing the word of God with the local shepherds. He also shared the food he prepared in a pot, and he used a bell to call the shepherds when the food was ready.

When the Romans threatened religious persecution, St Giles fled the valley. But before he left he hid the pot, the bell, the cross and the icon of the Virgin Mary that he had carved and painted. After a prophetic dream, a pilgrim called Amadéu started to search for the items in 1072. He built a chapel for pilgrims, and a few years later he found the objects.

Today they are kept in the Hermitage of St Giles, which was constructed during the 17th century on the site of the original chapel built by Amadéu. The Romanesque carving of Our Lady of Núria that is in the church was most probably made in the 12th or 13th century, and not in the 8th century.

In the summer the fantastic trails attract hikers, while in the winter the ski slopes offer a great getaway. A hotel, restaurant and shop cater for the visitors all year round.

WALK 24

Puigmal

Start/finish	Núria, N42.396363, E2.152557
Distance	9km (there and back)
Total ascent/descent	950m
Grade	3
Time	4hr
Refreshments	Café and restaurant in Núria.
Access	You can take the rack railway (Cramallera) to and from Núria from Queralbs or Ribes de Freser – book your tickets in advance: www.valldenuria.cat
Public transport	Rack railway from Queralbs or Ribes de Freser to Núria.

This straightforward route leads you to the highest mountain in the area, Puigmal. Some sections are steep and demanding but your efforts will be well rewarded with the far-reaching mountain views. Take the rack railway or – if time allows and you feel up for it – follow the Camí Vell de Núria from Queralbs to Núria (see Walk 23). You can also spend a couple of days in Núria and explore further trails in the area.

Looking back to the high mountains surrounding the valley

Facing the monastery, go left towards the stables. At L'ascensió al Puigmal trail information board keep right and walk alongside the stable buildings.

> Prior to 1931 when the rack railway started operating, **Vall de Núria** was only accessible on foot. Several pilgrimage routes were used to reach Núria.

Go left uphill on the narrow path after the buildings, climbing away from the **campsite** and the buildings of Núria. Shortly after, cross another path and continue straight on the path marked with yellow signs. Climb steeply uphill and away from Núria with great views all around.

Look out for the yellow signs on rocks on the grassy mountainside. Soon you can also see a rocky gorge on your right. Cross a stream in a gully and, after about

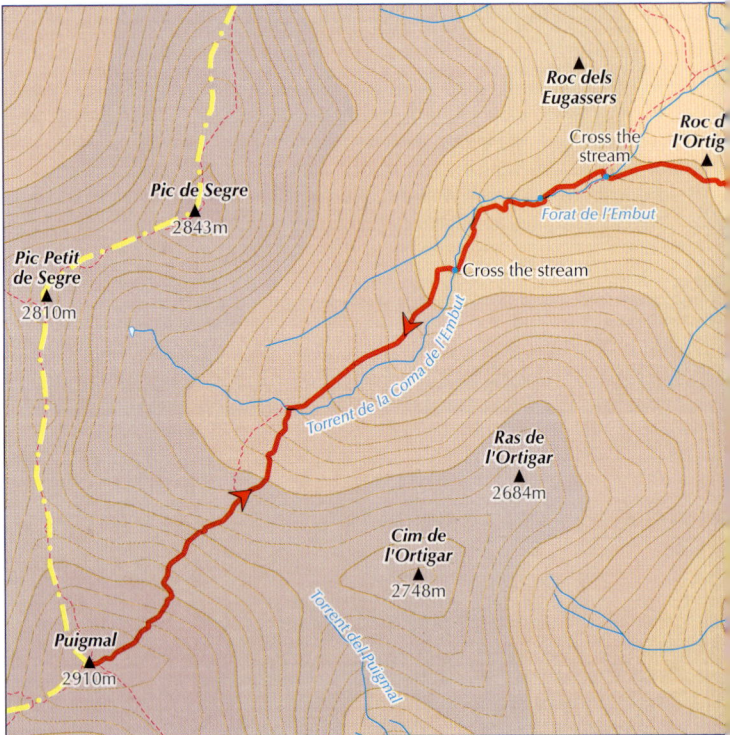

40min of steady uphill climb from Núria, reach a path junction with a signpost and go left towards Puigmal. Notice the distance and times given on the sign (3km, 1hr 30min) which suggest a difficult terrain ahead.

Follow the exposed path with the gully on the left and then ascend on the rocky mountainside. Pass **Forat de l'Embut** where the stream disappears beneath rocks and continue with the stream on your right. The path is marked with rock cairns. Cross the stream on rocks, then shortly after start to zigzag uphill with views towards the mountains. This is a steep section which feels long, but soon the cross on the top comes into view.

From the summit of **Puigmal** (alt. 2910m) enjoy the 360-degree panorama. Mountains fill the horizon as far as you can see. Only a few metres from the peak marker is the Spanish–French border. From the peak retrace your steps to Núria.

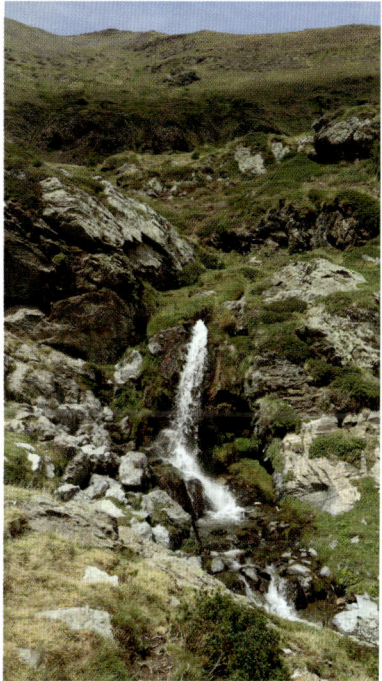

This stream has to be crossed a couple of times on the way

WALK 25
Pic de Finestrelles

Start/finish	Núria, N42.396363, E2.152557
Distance	12km
Total ascent/descent	910m
Grade	3
Time	5hr
Refreshments	Café, restaurant and shop in Núria.
Access	You can take the rack railway to Núria from Queralbs or Ribes de Freser. Book your tickets in advance: www. valldenuria.cat. There is also a hotel and a campsite where you can stay if you wish to spend a few days exploring the trails in the area.
Public transport	Rack railway from Queralbs or Ribes de Freser to Núria.

Tackle this route on a clear day and you will be spoilt with splendid views as you climb to the peak of Finestrelles. A section of the walk follows the ridge that runs along the French–Spanish border. The summer months are perfect if you want to spot playful marmots and chamois skilfully traversing the steep slopes of this unforgettable landscape.

Start by the stable building and walk towards the playground. Cross the river just after the animal pens and at the signpost go left and continue with the river on your left. At the **Santuari de Núria**, R112 junction, carry straight on alongside the river towards the mountains with the building behind you. Follow the wide path, passing the campsite on your left, and then continue alongside the ski lift (alternatively you can follow the path across the campsite, which will meet the other one just after the bridge). Your route is marked with red/white and yellow signs during this first section.

Cross the river on a **bridge** and continue uphill on the path marked with yellow signs. (There are two bridges close to each other; one is on the path coming from the campsite.) At the junction with a signpost keep right towards Finestrelles and then go left uphill on the rocky path near the closed concrete reservoir. Pass a small **waterfall** and cross Torrent de la Coma de l'Embut on rocks, then ascend on

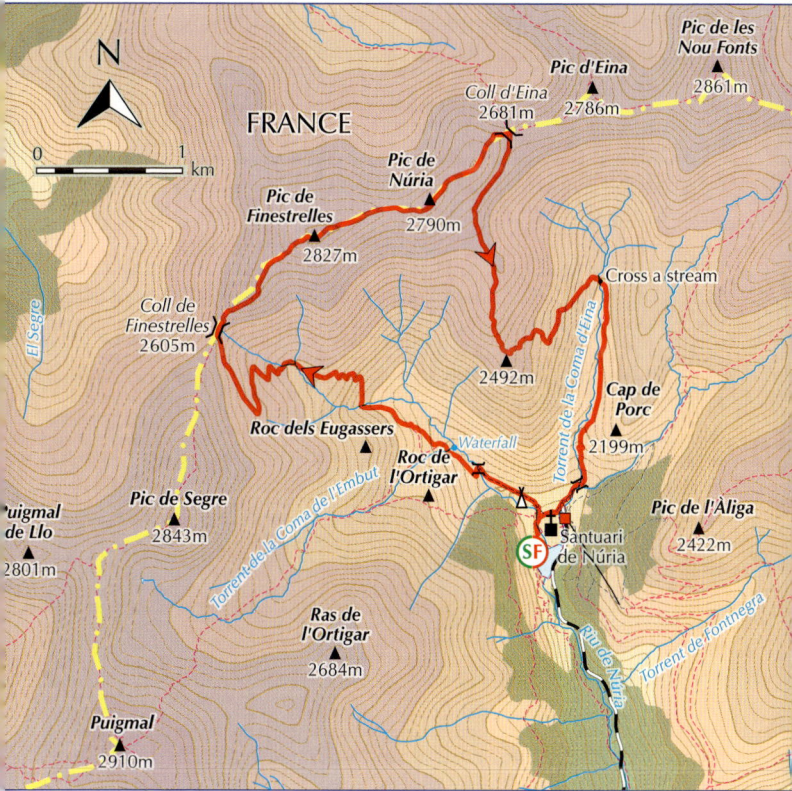

the grassy hillside with mountain views. At the junction with the signpost go right towards Finestrelles on the GR trail marked with red/white. (The path marked with yellow goes towards Puigmal to the left.)

Follow this path for about 1hr 30min to reach Coll de Finestrelles. Climb initially on the grassy slope. Cross a stream on rocks and zigzag steeply uphill, and then the path drops down to cross Torrent de Finestrelles before it bends right and climbs to **Coll de Finestrelles**.

At Coll de Finestrelles go right uphill on the narrow path. (From the col the GR trail continues down to France, and Puigmal is about 3km away to the left along the ridge.) Climb the steep rocky path with some great views for about

30min and reach **Pic de Finestrelles** (alt. 2827m). Like many other peaks along the ridge, Finestrelles is on the French–Spanish border. Enjoy the 360-degree panorama which encompasses an endless sea of mountains and long ridges. Núria is below and you can make out the peak of Puigmal, the highest mountain in the area.

From the peak continue on the narrow path with views towards the Núria valley below on the right. Descend and then follow the cairns on the ridge for about 30min to Puig de la coll d'Eina.

Descend and shortly notice a border marker with French signs. Reach **Coll d'Eina** and keep right. At the wooden signpost carry straight on towards Santuari de Núria (4.5km) and follow the red/white signs downhill with excellent views. Soon the ski slopes and buildings come into view as you zigzag downhill. Narrow streams race down on the grassy slopes, where you can see cattle grazing. Reach the bottom of the valley after descending for over an hour.

Cross a stream (Torrent de la Coma d'Eina) on rocks and keep right by the signpost on the GR path towards Núria. Walk with the river on your right and soon you will see the lake and the monastery of Núria. Cross a small **stone bridge** and head towards the buildings.

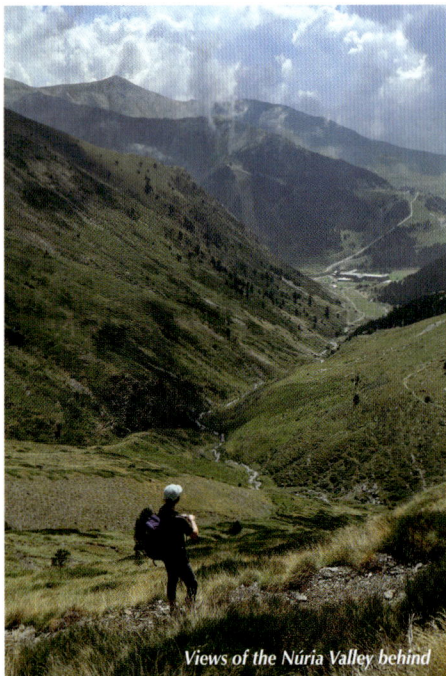

Views of the Núria Valley behind

WALK 26
Salt del Grill and Coma de Vaca

Start/finish	Queralbs, hydroelectric station, N42.362400, E2.174894
Distance	19km
Total ascent/descent	1530m
Grade	3
Time	8hr
Refreshment	Coma de Vaca
Access	Just before reaching Queralbs on the GIV-5217 road, turn right on a road marked towards Serrat, Fustanyà. Cross the bridge and carry straight on for 700 metres to a car park on the right.
Public transport	Take the rack railway to Queralbs and then from the station, walk about 1.5km to reach the hydroelectric power station where the trail starts.

This wonderful but demanding full-day walk takes you first to the impressive Salt del Grill waterfall, then along the narrow path to the Coma de Vaca refuge. The return route initially follows a section of the GR11 trail; this is exposed in places, so sure-footedness is required. The descent then continues on a lesser path marked only with rock cairns which are occasionally hard to spot; some route-finding skills are therefore required. This route can be made less demanding by retracing your steps from the refuge.

From the car park take the sealed road to the hydroelectric station, then cross the river on a **footbridge** by the signpost (Daió) and go right towards Cascada del Salt del Grill with the river on your right. Follow the rocky path uphill initially through woods. Just after 1km into the walk, reach the waterfall, **Salt del Grill**. Watch the water cascading down the vertical rock face, and then continue on the rocky path uphill, passing a memorial plaque. Ignore a path on the left with a helicopter sign. You will return on that path if you do the described full circular route.

Continue on the well-trodden path and at **Palanca de les Ribes**, R111 junction, carry straight on towards Refugi Coma de Vaca. From there follow the narrow path, first through woods then crossing a stream a couple of times on rocks. Climb uphill with more and more views of the towering mountains. Cross the

Narrow rocky path high above the river

River Freser on a **footbridge** then walk across a clearing and ascend with the river on your left. The path often runs on the exposed mountainside with some spectacular views to the Freser river gorge and the craggy mountains on the other side of the gorge. The refuge building comes into view after about 1hr 40min from the Palanca de les Ribes, R111 junction. The river is below on your left, and as the path bends away from the refuge building the views are once again dominated with grassy slopes. At **Torrent del Bogader**, R110 junction, go left downhill and cross a stream on rocks.

Follow the signs heading towards the refuge building. Cross the river on a footbridge and arrive at **Refugi Coma de Vaca** (alt. 2000m).

You can then either retrace your steps or continue on the 'Engineers Path' (Camí dels Enginyers), marked with red/white GR signs, on the left side of the building. Climb up and away from the building. Just across the gorge you can see the narrow path on the mountainside that you traversed on the way here. Towering mountains dominate the scenery as far as you can see. You will follow the narrow path marked with the red/white signs for nearly 3hr to Pedrisses, R229 junction.

This side of the gorge is more rugged and the rocky path is very exposed; sure-footedness is required in many places. There is a short, easy scramble where you might have to use your hands, and there are some short, aided sections with iron chains to hold on to. The path follows the contour of the mountainside with amazing views. Cross a stream that cuts through the grassy mountainside and soon the views open up towards Queralbs. You can also spot a stone building (**Refugi de les Pedrisses**) on the mountainside as the path levels, not long before you reach **Pedrisses**, R229 junction.

From the junction go left downhill on the faint, unmarked path (there is a path marked with an 'X' heading down towards a stone shelter). Descend, keeping slightly left, and locate some cairns in the depression. Follow the cairns downhill on the grassy slope, and soon the path becomes more distinguishable. It is important that you follow the cairns, as there are unmarked paths which are most probably used by cattle.

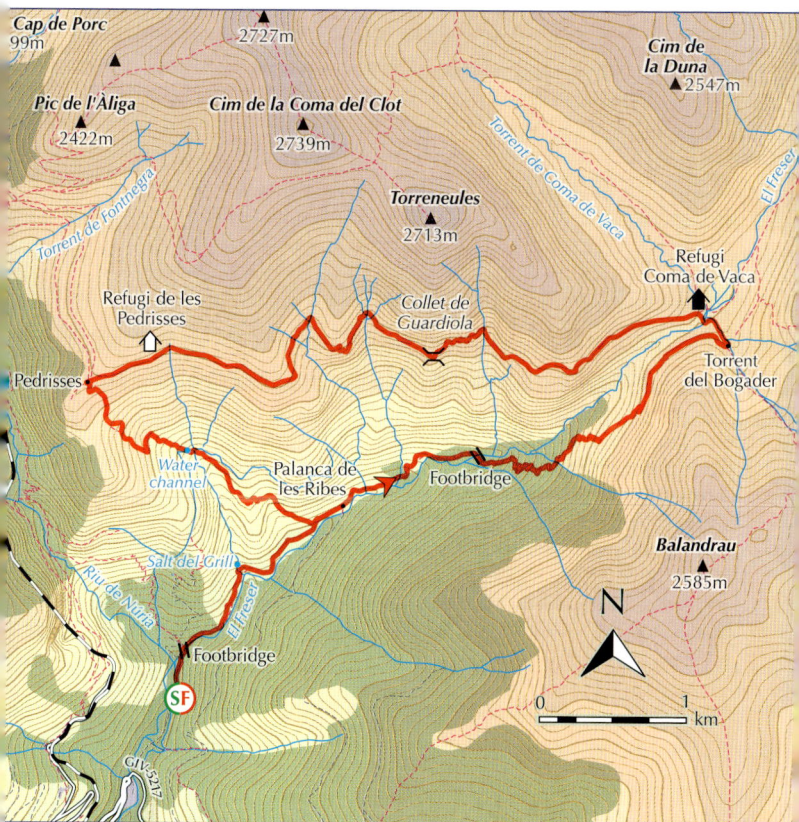

Refugi de Coma de Vaca at 2000m elevation

Descend on the mountainside with a trickling stream nearby and soon you see a man-made **water channel** tracing the contour of the mountainside below. The path then crosses the covered water channel and continues downhill. Cross a stream on rocks (Torrent del Salt del Grill) and descend steeply on the grassy mountainside with great mountain views. There is more and more vegetation. Passing a wire fence, descend among the bushes then zigzag downhill. After descending for 1hr 30min from Pedrisses, R229 junction, arrive back on the path heading towards the Coma de Vaca refuge (by the helicopter sign). Go right and retrace your steps to the car park.

WALK 27
Falgars and Roc de la Lluna

Start/finish	La Pobla de Lillet town hall, N42.243696, E1.974675
Distance	18km
Total ascent/descent	1030m
Grade	2
Time	5hr 30min
Refreshments	Café and restaurants in La Pobla de la Lillet; restaurant at Santuari de Santa Maria de Falgars.
Access	The village is located 9km east of Guardiola de Berguedà, along the B-402 road; car park near centre.
Public transport	Limited buses from Bagà.

The trail described initially follows a section of the GR4 and then the PR-C 52 signposted routes, but your route occasionally joins other paths that criss-cross the mountains. This long route runs on easy terrain across the Serra del Catllaràs mountains and enables you to enjoy some fine views while traversing the forested mountains.

Start from the town hall and cross the bridge over the Llobregat River. Leaving Camí de l'Escorxador, take the narrow GR4.2 marked path to the left uphill. Shortly after, reach a road and keep left. About 50 metres later take the path on the right and cross a sealed road near the heliport. Continue straight alongside a woodland adventure park and at the path junction at the end of the adventure park go left uphill. Keep left on the track and then 20 metres later go right uphill on a path.

At El Tinar junction continue on the GR4 Falgars (pels graus) route straight on. Ignore any unmarked paths as you walk alongside fields and ascend with the village behind you. At the next junction with signpost take the GR4 marked path towards Falgars to the right. Follow the rocky path with some views to the nearby mountains; shortly after, cross a **stone bridge**.

At the path junction turn left and then follow the red/white signs immediately right, and then – when the path splits – keep right. About 1hr 20min from the village emerge from the forest by an electricity pole and head towards the church building, passing **Mirador Joan Casanova** (viewpoint). Reach a tarmac road; the route continues to the left, but first make a short detour to the church, **Santa Maria**

117

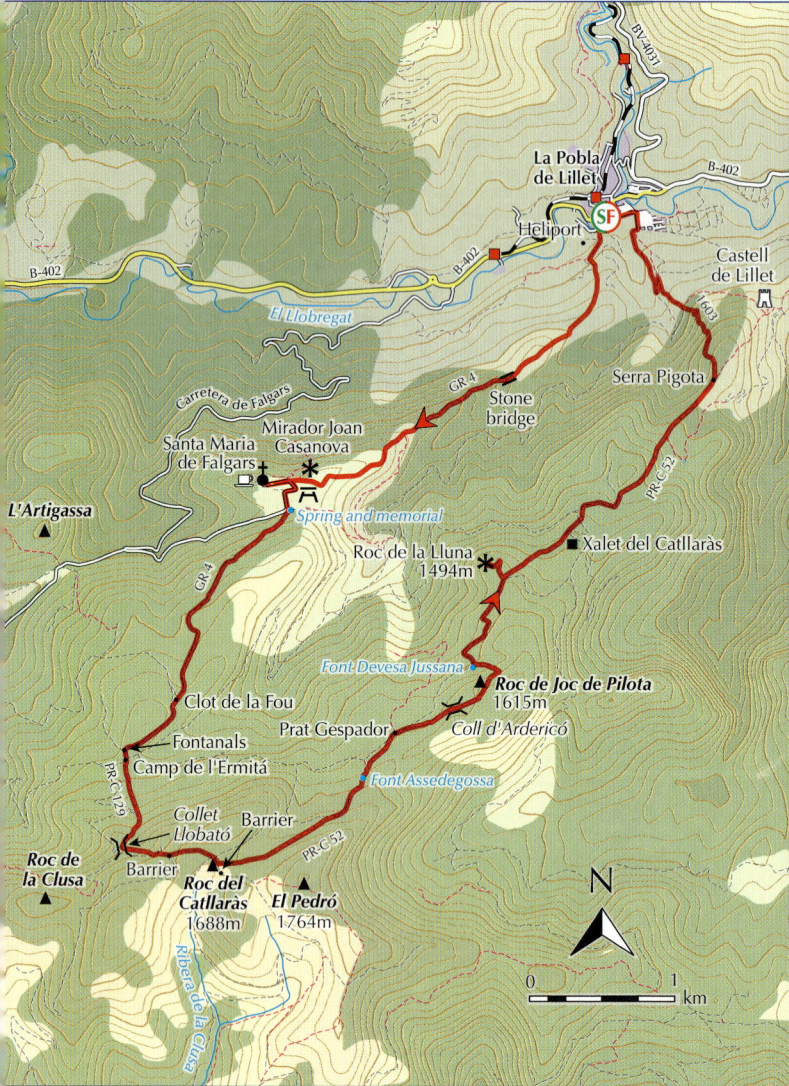

BV-4031

La Pobla de Lillet

B-402

Heliport

SF

Castell de Lillet

1603

Serra Pigota

B-402

El Llobregat

GR 4

Stone bridge

PR-C-52

Carretera de Falgars

Mirador Joan Casanova

Santa Maria de Falgars

L'Artigassa

Spring and memorial

Roc de la Lluna 1494m

Xalet del Catllaràs

GR 4

Font Devesa Jussana

Roc de Joc de Pilota 1615m

Clot de la Fou

Prat Gespador

Coll d'Ardericó

Fontanals

Camp de l'Ermitá

Font Assedegossa

PR-C-129

Collet Llobató

Barrier

PR-C-52

Roc de la Clusa

Barrier

Roc del Catllaràs 1688m

El Pedró 1764m

Ribera de la Clusa

N

0   1 km

de Falgars, to the right. There is also a hostel and a restaurant in the building, and there is a picnic site nearby.

> The **Falgars Sanctuary** is dedicated to the Virgin of Falgars as, according to legend, its statue was found in a nearby cave. The original building dates back to 1049 and the current building is from 1646. It has also operated as a guest house since the 1930s: www.falgars.com.

Follow the road downhill to Collada de Falgars road junction. Cross over to the **spring and memorial**, and continue behind the spring on a path to the right uphill. Reach a track, keep right and a few metres later go left on the path marked with red/white signs. Shortly after, reach a forest track at a track junction, follow the signs to the right and then immediately go left.

At the junction take the path on the left uphill, ignoring any paths marked with an 'X'. At the big forest track junction take the second track from the right uphill; ignore any unmarked path and follow red/white signs. At **Clot de la Fou** go left towards Collet Llobató.

There are PR-C 129 yellow/white signs, as well as red/white GR signs. At **Fontanals junction** follow the PR-C 129 route straight on, and shortly after at **Camp de l'Ermità** carry straight on towards Collet Llobató. Ascend steeply alongside a wire fence and get close to a track as you follow yellow/white markers. About an hour from Collada de Falgars road junction, emerge from the woods on to a track at **Collet Llobató**. Take the PR-C 52 route to the left and almost immediately go left on a path (wooden sign towards Casa Refugi), and soon you will see yellow/white signs. Reach a track, keep left and a few metres later go right uphill on a path. Shortly after, arrive back on the track and go right. Descend gently, ignoring a track on the right with a barrier (conservation area).

At a clearing, head towards the information boards, ignoring a track on the right and then one on the left. Arrive at **Roc del Catllaràs** by the wildlife reserve area and its information boards. Leave the track to the right just before the barrier and follow the yellow/white signs through the forest.

Join a track and keep right as it soon becomes a path. Pass a spring, **Font Assedegossa**. At a clearing join a track by another spring, Font de Prat Gespador, and keep right on the track by the Prat Gespador signpost (ignore the other PR-C 11 route on the left leaving the track).

Follow the PR-C 52 route towards La Pobla de Lillet with views ahead to the rocky peak of Roc de Joc de Pilota (alt. 1615m) with a cross. Take the narrow path on the right, leaving the track, and ascend through forest. Emerge from the forest and cross the clearing, heading towards a signpost. At the edge of the clearing at **Coll d'Ardericó** keep left towards La Pobla de Lillet.

Idyllic path across pines at Roc del Catllaràs

Viewpoint at Roc de la Lluna with the impressive Pedraforca in the distance

Descend through forest ignoring a path marked with an 'X'. Follow the rocky path sharply left downhill and soon you have some great views towards the mountains, including Pedraforca. Reach a track by a spring (**Font Devesa Jussana**) and go right. Descend, following the track and passing the ruins of a building. About 1hr 20min from the wildlife reserve make the short detour to the viewpoint at **Roc de la Lluna** (alt. 1494m) on the left. From the viewing platform the mountains of the Cadí-Moixeró fill the horizon as far as you can see.

Return towards the track, but just before reaching it take the narrow path on the left downhill. Crossing another path continue straight on downhill with some mountain views. Soon pass **Xalet del Catllaràs** and follow the yellow/white signs straight on by the stone building on the left.

The wealthy industrialist Eusebi Güell commissioned the construction of **Xalet del Catllaràs** – designed by Gaudi in 1902 – to house the technicians and engineers of Catllaràs coal mines.

La Pobla de Lillet and the peaks of Cadí-Moixeró behind

The building was donated to the council in 1932, and by 1940 it was in a very poor condition. In 1971 it was renovated and used as a youth summer camp for some years, but as some regulations changed in the late 1980s it once again fell into disrepair. Currently the building is undergoing renovation.

Reach and cross a forest track and continue straight on the PR-C 52 towards La Pobla de Lillet. Shortly after, arrive on another forest track and go right, and then 50 metres later at the junction go right. At the next junction with a signpost keep left (Terra Negra junction).

At **Serra Pigota junction** go left downhill towards La Pobla de Lillet, then follow the yellow signs of the 1603 route (the PR-C 52 continues straight on). As you descend steeply the village comes into view. Zigzag down to and cross a track and continue on the path downhill. Reach and cross another track and continue downhill.

On reaching a track by a house continue straight on alongside the fence. Descend on the track towards the village, reach a gravel track and go left. In the sharp right-hand bend the track becomes a sealed road; keep right downhill on this road. Reach the outskirts of the village at Les Coromines junction and follow the yellow/white signs passing the 14th-century bridge into the centre of the village.

CADÍ-MOIXERÓ NATURAL PARK

Pedraforca views from the demanding steep trail to Comabona (Walk 34)

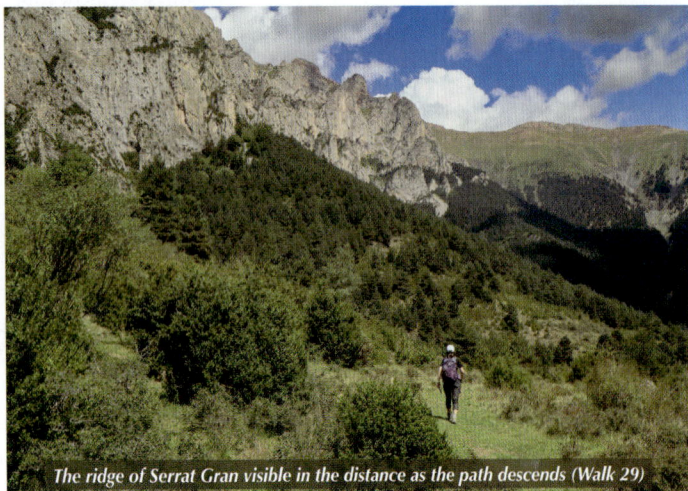

The ridge of Serrat Gran visible in the distance as the path descends (Walk 29)

The Cadí-Moixeró Natural Park was established in 1983 in the Pre-Pyrenees, and there are numerous marked trails criss-crossing these mountains. Climb Penyes Altes de Moixeró (Walk 29) or La Tosa (Walk 28) to enjoy some extensive views. However, the most challenging – and yet the busiest – route in the area is the demanding climb to the peak of Pedraforca (Walk 32). The iconic forked mountain, which is separate from the range, is believed to be one of the most photographed mountains in Catalunya.

Climb Comabona (Walk 34) or take the peaceful Pedraforca 360 trail (Walk 35) if you want to enjoy some stunning views of Pedraforca without climbing the popular mountain.

Bagà or Guardiola de Berguadà, which have shops and restaurants, could be good bases to explore the area. If you'd prefer to stay in a smaller, quieter place, you can also find accommodation in Saldes or Gósol; both villages cater to walkers and are located at the foot of Pedraforca. There are also plenty of good campsites dotted around.

WALK 28

La Tosa

Start/finish	Trencapinyes car park, N42.291291, E1.886726
Distance	16km
Total ascent/descent	1300m
Grade	3
Time	6hr
Refreshments	Snack bar at the ski station on La Tosa; you can also get refreshments at Refugi de Rebost.
Access	The car park is located 14km north of Bagà on the BV-4024 road.

This great route in the Cadí-Moixeró Natural Park makes use of a combination of waymarked trails. Impressive views accompany you as you climb La Tosa (or La Tossa d'Alp) and follow the Moixeró ridge. In the summer La Tosa is a popular hiking area, while in the winter its ski slopes come to life.

From the car park take the path on the right uphill behind the map board just after the cattle grid. (There are yellow as well as orange signs.) Ascend through pine forest, and then across a grassy area that is also used for grazing cattle. The iconic shape of Pedraforca is behind you and the Moixeró ridge is on your left. Around 1km from the start cross a **track** by a signpost and continue on the path on its other side. Follow the orange signs through pine forest and then on the grassy mountainside with views of La Tossa and the valley below. When the narrow path splits keep slightly right uphill on the path marked with orange signs. Climb towards the barren top with some excellent views towards the rugged ridge across the valley.

At **Collada de Comafloriu** (alt. 2196m) follow the orange signs towards the mountain and shortly after the ski station comes into view. There are also views all the way to Pedraforca on the left. Ignore any unmarked paths and paths marked with an 'X'. As you follow the orange signs, you can also see some red/white GR signs. After an ascent through a rocky section to **Cap del Serrat Gran** (alt. 2402m) the path drops down to **Colladeta de Comabella** (alt. 2348m) before it climbs again. The buildings of the La Molina ski resort are visible below on the right.

As the ski station of La Tosa comes into view, head towards the building, passing some animal sculptures along the way. The ski lifts operate throughout the summer months, making La Tosa (alt. 2536m) a very busy mountaintop. Arrive at the **ski station** a little over 2hr from the car park. The route continues west towards Coll de Jou near the building by the viewpoint. Descend with great views towards Penyes Altes de Moixeró. There are red/white GR signs as well as the orange signs. Cross another path – the Miner's Trail – and continue on the GR path heading west along the narrow ridge. Descend steeply on the mountainside with views of the valley below. You can see Penyes Altes, and you can also make out Pedraforca and Comabona peaks in the distance.

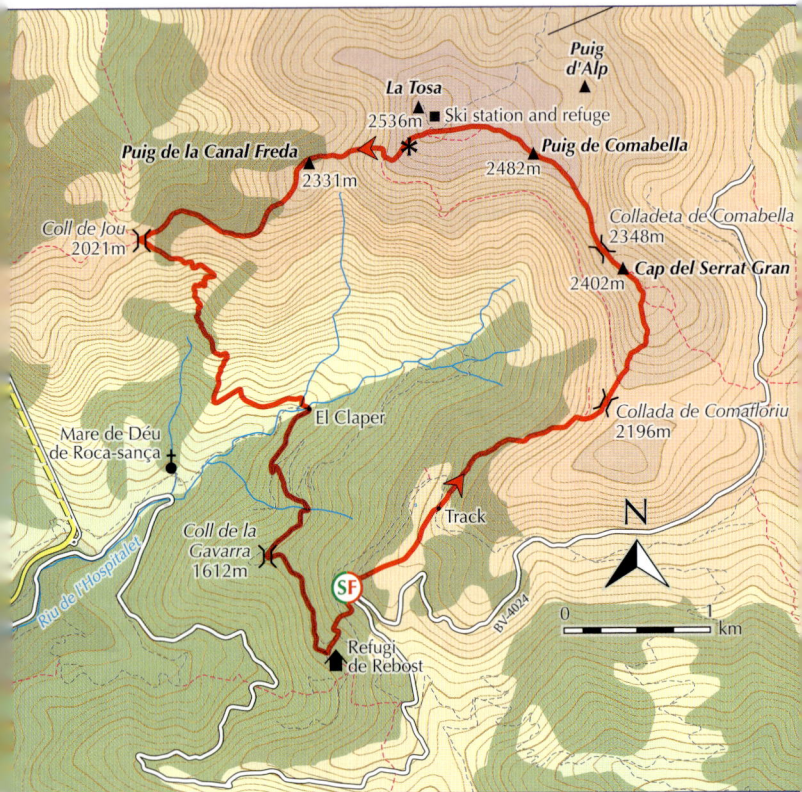

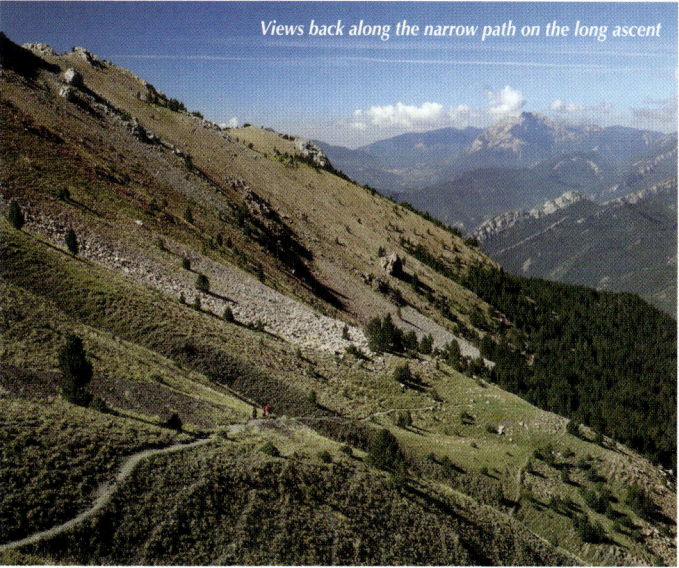

Views back along the narrow path on the long ascent

About an hour from the ski station arrive at **Coll de Jou** (alt. 2021m) and keep left downhill towards Refugi de Rebost. Follow the yellow/white signs, zigzagging downhill through forest for about an hour with some views, occasionally getting close to a rock wall, and reach **El Claper** path junction. Go left towards Refugi de Rebost on the PR-C 126 route and follow it on the mountainside with views of the towering mountains. Ignore a path marked with an 'X' on the left and follow the path bending sharply right. Reach a track and keep left uphill with the river on the right. Shortly after, leave the track to the right on a path uphill marked with a yellow/white sign.

After a steep ascent reach the track and keep right uphill ignoring a track with a barrier on the left. A few minutes later leave the track to the left uphill and shortly reach the track again at **Coll de la Gavarra** (alt. 1612m). Go left on the track and at the junction keep right downhill towards Refugi de Rebost through a barrier. Shortly after, arrive at **Refugi de Rebost** and climb some steps on the left to a signpost. Keep left uphill towards Mirador dels Orris. Pass a spring and trough, and shortly after reach and cross a track. Follow the orange signs uphill passing a spring, Font Ramon Espel. Cross a GR path and continue straight on uphill to arrive back at the car park.

WALK 29

Penyes Altes de Moixeró

Start/finish	Gréixer, parking area alongside the BV-4024 road, N42.281032, E1.849101
Distance	17km
Total ascent/descent	1350m
Grade	3
Time	6hr 30min
Refreshments	None along the way.
Access	There is a parking area 4km north of Bagà alongside the BV-4024 road at Gréixer, shortly before it goes under the C-16 motorway viaduct.

This delightful but demanding route takes you to the peak of Penyes Altes de Moixeró, which – on a clear day – offers a breathtaking panorama of the mountains of the Cadí-Moixeró Natural Park. The trail described uses a combination of signposted trails, such as a section of a long-distance GR150–1 route and a shorter PR-C 126 route. The long climb to the summit is followed by a descent to Coll de Jou, where a steep but rewarding path drops down to L'Hospitalet de Roca-sança.

Leave the BV-4024 road on the track uphill towards Penyes Altes de Moixeró (5.7km). As you go through a barrier you can enjoy the first great mountain views. Walk alongside fields and ignore the track going towards the houses of **Gréixer** on the right. Leave the sealed track to the left towards Penyes Altes de Moixeró and at the junction with a signpost go on the Camí de la Canal de la Serp route towards Penyes Altes. Pass above the houses and leave the track on a path to the left uphill towards Penyes Altes. Shortly after, climb with views of the nearby mountains. For a couple of kilometres you follow the yellow signs mostly uphill through forest with some views, occasionally near a sheer rock face.

Ascend on the more exposed grassy hillside and look out for cairns as well as yellow signs painted on rocks. After a climb of about 2hr 30min, arrive at **Coll de Raset** and go right towards Penyes Altes on the GR150–1 trail. Follow the red/white signs among pines just below the ridge. Climb on rocks where you might

have to use your hands. Ignore any other unmarked paths and follow the markers on rocks. Near the peak – just before the path starts to descend – keep right to the summit of **Penyes Altes de Moixeró** (alt. 2276m), where you can enjoy the 360-degree panorama. From the peak return to the GR path and descend, following the red/white signs. At the signpost continue straight on towards Coll de Jou. Spot the building of the ski station on the nearby La Tosa as you descend.

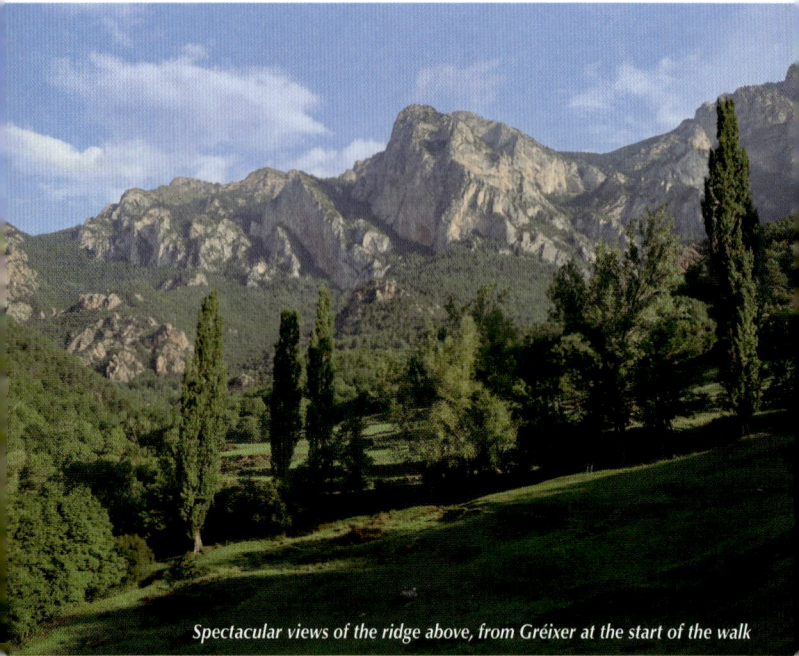

Spectacular views of the ridge above, from Gréixer at the start of the walk

Arrive at **Coll de Jou** (alt. 2021m) about an hour from the peak. Go right downhill on the PR-C 126 route and follow the yellow/white signs for about an hour through forest with some views, occasionally getting close to a rock wall. Reach a path junction with the overgrown ruins of a building at **El Claper**.

Go right on the yellow 1006 route towards L'Hospitalet de Roca-sança. After about 30min of descent arrive at a church and a farm – this is **L'Hospitalet de Roca-sança**. The yellow marked route takes you across the farmyard to reach a tarmac road. Turn right and follow the tarmac road for 3km back to the starting point.

WALK 30
Els Empedrats

Start/finish	Els Empedrats car park, N42.268136, E1.815067
Distance	11.5km
Total ascent/descent	820m
Grade	2
Time	4hr 30min
Refreshments	Refugi Vents del Cadí; Refugi Sant Jordi
Access	The Els Empedrats car park is located 4.2km west of Bagà along the Camí de Monell road. The road becomes gravel track near the Pont de Sant Joan picnic site. There are limited places to park near the guest house by the river, but there are more spaces along the road farther back.

This signposted PR-C 125 route initially follows an impressive rocky gorge, crossing the river several times and passing Els Empedrats waterfall. The route also follows a short section of the old paved route that used to connect the north and south of Moixeró through Coll de Pendís. The second part of the trail climbs away from the river through a ridge and then descends steeply with fantastic views towards Pedraforca.

The restored 17th-century building (l'Hostalet) of Refugi Vents del Cadí

At the track junction near the building just after the bridge, go right on the track towards Els Empedrats. Pass the restored 17th-century hostel, **Refugi Vents del Cadí**, and then with the river on your right follow the yellow/white marked path through forest and then on rocks.

At the junction with a signpost the route continues to the right, but first follow the path on the left to **Bullidor de la Llet waterfall**. Return to the junction and go left towards Empedrats. The gorge narrows and you walk on the remains of an old, cobbled route. Soon cross the river on rocks and then keep left upstream on rocks following the yellow/white signs. The dramatic, narrow gorge, with towering rocks above, dominates the landscape. About 30–40min from the refuge cross the river on rocks by the waterfall, **Els Empedrats**, and then climb on rocks passing the waterfall from above. Continue in the riverbed among boulders and before long cross the river on rocks again. Follow the yellow/white signs uphill as the path bends slightly away from the river.

The gorge narrows down, forcing the water to run faster between rocks. Zigzag uphill following the yellow/white signs and cross the river again. The path widens and, about 45min from Els Empedrats, pass **Font Gran d'Escriu**. Cross a stream on rocks and then ascend through forest away from the gorge. Climb the grassy hillside and, just before you reach Font del Faig junction, follow the yellow/

Cap de la Boixassa viewed from Pas de Galigan

white signs to the left (for Refugi Sant Jordi, go right from Font del Faig junction). Shortly after, pass **Font del Faig** (spring) and then continue uphill through forest with some views of the rugged mountains on the left. Pass by a rock face and then shortly after the views open up as you follow the narrow ridge.

There are also some views towards the gorge below, and to Penyes Altes on the left. Fascinating rock formations dominate the landscape on the right. Before long Pedraforca comes into view. About 30–40min from Font del Faig keep left on the ridge for 50 metres and then drop down to the right. Descend for about 30min with incredible views towards Pedraforca. Arrive on a track at **Coll de la Pelosa** and continue on its other side downhill. A few minutes later reach a track and keep right downhill, and 100 metres later leave the track to the left on a path. Follow the rocky path downhill and soon pass by a rock wall. Descend the rough, rocky path to a track; keep left and a few metres later leave the track on the yellow/white path up on the left. Shortly after, arrive back on a track by the map board near **Refugi Vents del Cadí**. Go left and over the bridge, and arrive back at the parking area.

WALK 31
Via del Nicolau

Start/finish	Plaça de l'Església, Guardiola de Berguedà, N42.232636, E1.879416
Distance	12.5km (there and back)
Total ascent/descent	430m
Grade	1
Time	3hr 30min
Refreshments	Café, restaurant and shop in Guardiola de Berguedà; spring near San Joan de l'Avellanet picnic site.
Access	Guardiola de Berguedà is located along the C-16 road 20km north of Berga – there are plenty of parking places at Plaça de l'Església
Public transport	Buses from Berga.

This there-and-back trail follows the route of the old railway line that was constructed at the beginning of the 20th century to transport wood. The well-restored and well-maintained footpath runs through tunnels and across bridges, including a suspension bridge to San Joan de l'Avellanet picnic site, where you can visit the nearby 12th-century church.

VIA DEL NICOLAU

A railway – promoted by Tomàs Nicolau I Prieto, owner of the sawmill in Berga – was built between 1914 and 1916 to transport wood to Guardiola de Berguedà. Tunnels and bridges were built to navigate through the mountainous landscape. However, after only a few years, the railway was abandoned and rapidly deteriorated. A huge restoration work was carried out in 2009, and a path suitable for cycling, walking and running was made.

Follow the signs (which show a picture of a log cart) for the Via del Nicolau trail from the roundabout, heading towards Bagà. Cross the Bastareny river on the bridge and a few minutes later go left by the signpost. Follow the paved road and

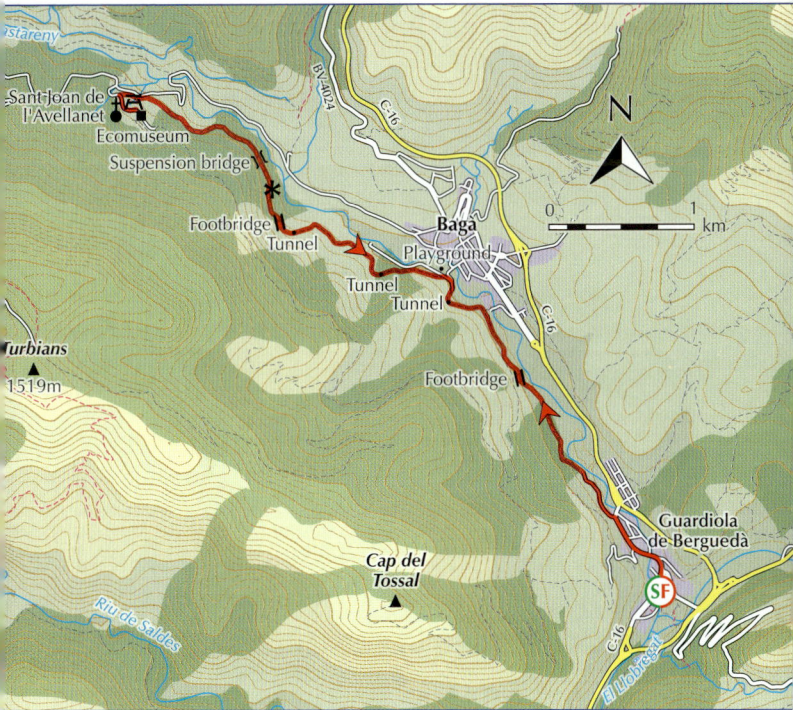

when it splits take the left branch passing some houses. The road then becomes a path by the last house. Follow the well-trodden signposted forest path, ignoring any other paths. Crossing a wooden footbridge, reach a tarmac road and keep right. Ignore a joining road on the right and continue straight on, passing a viewpoint where you can enjoy some views of Bagà and the mountains behind.

Go through a **tunnel** and ignore the road going down to Bagà on the right. About 80 metres later (just before arriving at a playground) leave the tarmac road to the left. There are views towards Bagà and more mountain views in front of you. Shortly after, enter the next **tunnel**. For about 30min follow the route on the mountainside through another longer **tunnel** and over bridges. Pass a viewpoint and reach a long **suspension bridge**.

Continue on a forest path and after a short ascent reach a tarmac road near the San Joan de l'Avellanet picnic site. Go left on the tarmac road, and shortly

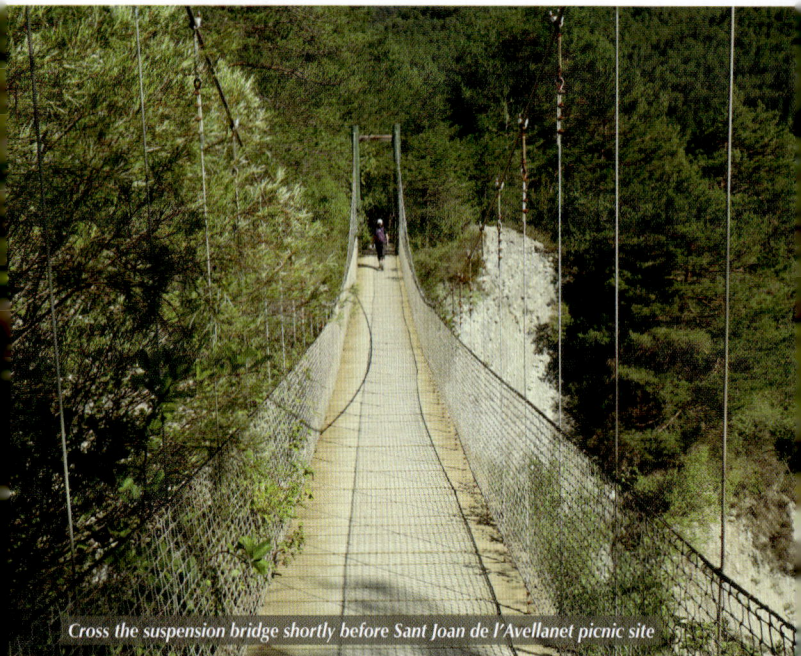

Cross the suspension bridge shortly before Sant Joan de l'Avellanet picnic site

after pass a spring and take the narrow path on the right that climbs to the 12th-century Romanesque-style **Sant Joan de l'Avellanet Church**. You can also follow the tarmac road for a few more metres to the building that houses the **ecomuseum** (at the time of going to print, the museum is currently closed).

WALK 32

Pedraforca Superior

Start/finish	Mirador de Gresolet, N42.247200, E1.722680
Distance	8.5km
Total ascent/descent	1160m
Grade	3+
Time	5hr 30min
Refreshments	Refreshments at Refugi Lluís Estasen.
Access	From the B-400 road near Saldes take the narrow Carrer del Mirador del Gresolet road to Mirador de Gresolet; there is a car park at the viewpoint.
Public transport	There is a bus service from Gósol and Saldes to the viewpoint (www.buspedraforca.com); seek information in the villages.

Despite its long scrambling section, this classic signposted walk is a very popular route to Pedraforca Pollegó Superior, the highest peak of Pedraforca. Because of the challenging terrain, only attempt to climb Pedraforca in good weather conditions and make sure you leave early, as you need the better part of a day to cover the distance.

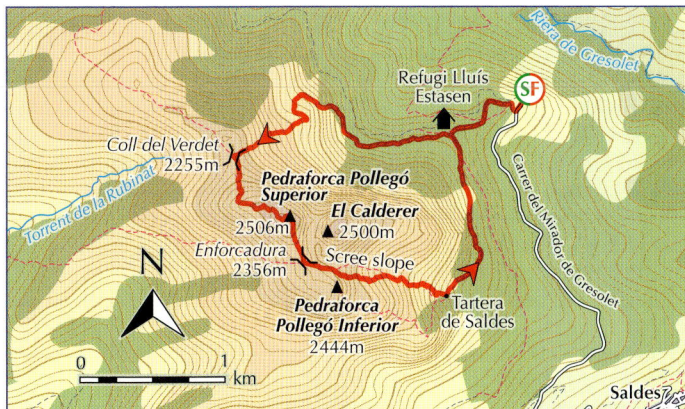

Steep descent to the gap (Enforcadura) with views of Gósol in the valley

From the car park at the Gresolet viewpoint walk back about 100 metres on the tarmac road and then take the path on the right up on steps. Follow the forest path marked with yellow/white stripes mainly uphill, ignoring any paths marked with an 'X'. It is a very popular trail, so try to stick to the marked path to minimise your impact. Arrive at **Refugi Lluís Estasen** about 10min from the car park. At the junction with a signpost by the refuge building, keep right and then (after the building) follow the yellow/white signs straight on on a well-trodden path as the rugged rocks of Pedraforca tower above you. You often have to clamber over rocks as you ascend through forest. The path then levels with some views on your right. Navigate between boulders and then zigzag steeply uphill. Notice the 'Pedraforca 2.5km 2hr 30min' sign; this time estimate is accurate, given the often challenging terrain. Look out for the yellow/white signs, keep left on the rocks and climb the narrow path with often amazing views. Climb steeply through forest with views towards the nearby mountains.

After about 1hr 10min climb from the refuge to reach **Coll del Verdet** (alt. 2255m). From the col enjoy some views towards Gósol and keep left towards the towering rocks. Follow the path for about 10min and reach the rocks with the yellow sign. This is where the scrambling starts, and from here it takes about an hour to reach the peak. This is not a very technical climb and there are lots of handholds; however, take extra care and give space to others. Keep an eye out for the yellow markers so you won't stray off the route. Scramble up on rocks and then follow the ridge. Drop down a little before scrambling farther up on the rocks again, then drop slightly down again before the final scramble up to the peak. From **Pedraforca Pollegó Superior** (alt. 2506m) enjoy the truly amazing and well-deserved 360-degree panorama. On a clear day you can see the jagged mountains of the Montserrat and Montseny ranges in the distance. The immediate scenery is dominated by the second peak, El Calderer (alt. 2500m), and the lower peak, Pedraforca Pollegó Inferior (alt. 2444m), across the col.

From the peak descend in the direction of Pollegó Inferior. Drop steeply down following the yellow signs on rocks towards the col between the two peaks. This eventually becomes a rocky path and reaches **Enforcadura** (alt. 2356m) about 20min from the peak. Keep left and follow the yellow/white signs downhill through the scree (tartera). The steep, rough path swings closer to the rock face on the right. It is important that you stick to the marked path on the scree slope. This rough landscape is an important habitat for many creatures. Zigzag steeply downhill with some great views towards Saldes. As you get lower there are more trees and soon you walk on loose stones. After descending from Enforcadura for just over an hour, arrive at **Tartera de Saldes junction** and continue straight on towards the refuge. Continue on loose stones and then the path evens for a while on the mountainside. There are more shrubs and trees, and it is less steep as you descend. The path runs on the edge and then crosses two scree slopes which cut through the forest. At a junction with signs continue straight on towards the refuge. When you reach **Refugi Lluís Estasen**, keep right and retrace your steps back to the car park.

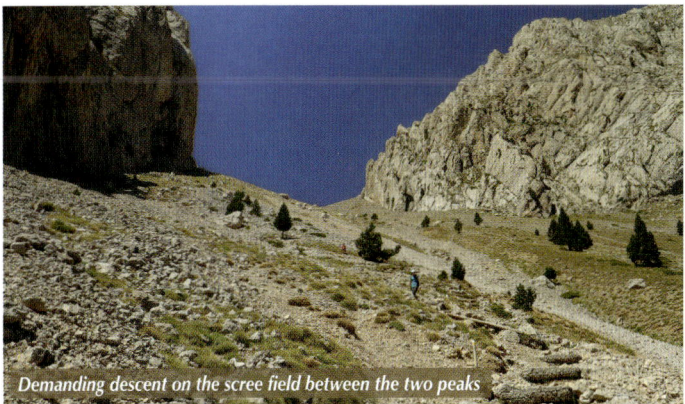

Demanding descent on the scree field between the two peaks

WALK 33
Saldes to Gresolet

Start/finish	Saldes town hall, N42.228628, E1.735161
Distance	13km
Total ascent/descent	680m
Grade	2
Time	4hr–4hr 30min
Refreshments	Café, restaurant and shop in Saldes; refreshments at Refugi del Gresolet.
Access	Saldes is located on the G-400 road about 18km east of Guardiola de Berguedà.
Public transport	Buses from Berga and Bagà.

From Saldes the green/white signposted trail takes you first to the ruins of the 12th-century Castell de Saldes just above the village and then to Santuari de Gresolet, tucked away in the valley. Remarkable views accompany you on this easy walk. From the sanctuary return alongside the river in the gorge before arriving back at Saldes.

Facing the town hall and information centre, keep right towards the church passing restaurants and cafés. Pass the church, Església de Sant Martí de Saldes, on your left and follow the green/white signs downhill. At the signpost go left towards Gresolet on 'Camí de Saldes a Coll de la Bena'. At the next signpost keep left towards Castell de Saldes (number 2 route) up on a stony path by the old barn. After a short but steep climb arrive on a track by a house and keep right. A few metres later leave the track to the left on a path towards Castell de Saldes and, at the junction near another house, take the narrow path with the house on your right going above the building. Shortly after reach the ruins of **Castell de Saldes**. Explore the ruins and enjoy some of the first views of the forked peaks of Pedraforca.

> The 12th-century **Castell de Saldes**, with its small 13th-century Santa Maria del Castell chapel, is located at the foot of Pedraforca overlooking the valley below.

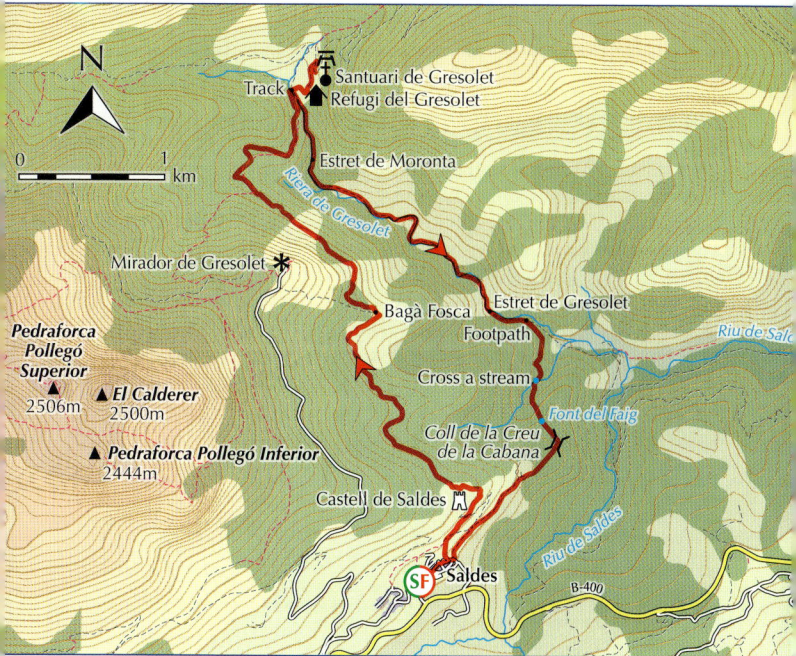

From the ruins, continue on the green/white marked path downhill. Descend on the broad path through forest ignoring any unmarked paths. There are occasional views to the Gresolet valley and Pedraforca when the trees thin out. After a steep descent the path levels for a while. When its splits, take the left branch with green/white sign slightly uphill (the other path drops down to the forest track). The path then gets close to the forest track and runs mainly parallel to it. About 30min from the castle ruins, reach a track and go left uphill. Shortly after at the junction follow the green/white signs left uphill, and almost immediately at the next junction keep right towards Gresolet. Walk through forest initially, and then with views to the mountains on your right and with Pedraforca towering behind you. Soon you can spot the church and the refuge building on the other side of the gorge. At **Bagà Fosca junction** continue straight on towards Gresolet. Cross the river on rocks, continue uphill and shortly after cross the river on rocks again. As well as green/white signs, you can see some orange signs on this section.

After a descent cross the river on rocks then reach and cross a track and follow the path to **Refugi del Gresolet**, and then on to **Santuari de Gresolet**. There is a picnic site by the church.

SANTUARI DE GRESOLET

According to legend a young shepherd lost a bull from his herd. When he found the bull, it was staring at an image (probably a carving). The shepherd put it in his bag and took it to the church of the castle of Saldes; however, when he arrived his bag was empty. He returned to the place in Gresolet to find the image miraculously back at its original place. He built the first chapel on that spot.

The church that stood in Gresolet was destroyed and rebuilt several times over the centuries, and part of the current church existed as early as 1709. The sanctuary was in the care of hermits between 1660 and 1959, and in 1959 the image of the Virgin Mary was moved to Saldes. Due to the poor state of the building, it has not been possible to enter the church since 2014.

From the picnic site follow the track back to the point where you crossed it and continue straight on along the track towards Saldes, or retrace your steps back to the track you crossed and keep left towards Saldes. Cross the river over a bridge in a narrow part of the gorge (**Estret de Moronta**) and follow this track for about 30min mostly alongside the river, ignoring any other tracks with some great views of the imposing Pedraforca.

Cross the River Gresolet on a bridge at another narrow section (**Estret de Gresolet**), and shortly after leave the track on the right on a footpath towards Saldes marked with a green/white sign.

Views of the refuge building and Pedraforca in the background

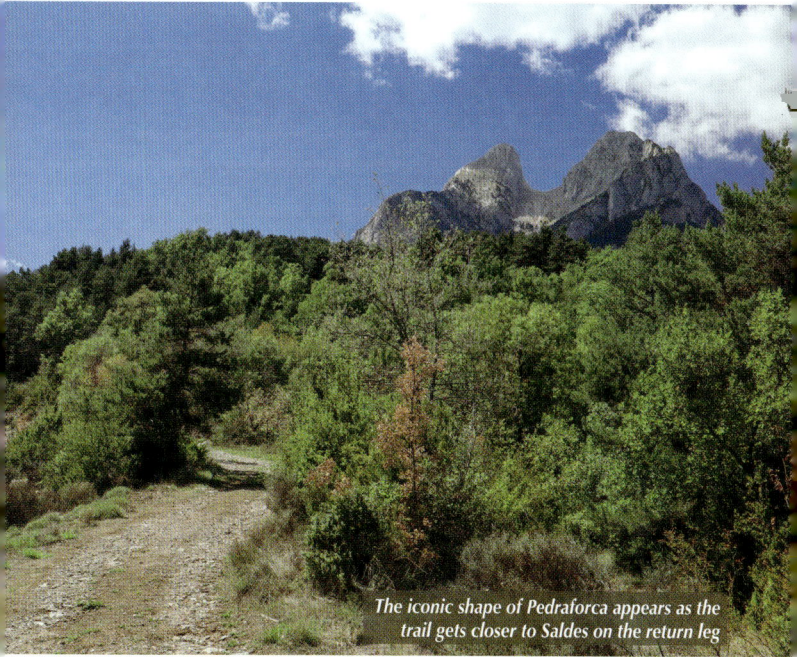

The iconic shape of Pedraforca appears as the trail gets closer to Saldes on the return leg

Ascend through forest and then on the mountainside with some views of the forested slopes. Cross a stream on rocks and as you zigzag uphill the magnificent Pedraforca occasionally comes into view. Pass a trough and then walk alongside a grassy area used for grazing. At **Coll de la Creu de la Cabana junction** go right on the forest track towards Saldes. Ignore a track marked with an 'X' on the right and continue straight on. The track becomes a surfaced road, and when you reach another track go left, ignoring a track on the right. At the next junction go left towards the church tower, then take the first street on the right. Climb the stairs and continue straight on back to the starting point passing Església de Sant Martí de Saldes.

WALK 34
Comabona

Start/finish	Santuari de Gresolet picnic site, N42.259016, E1.725050
Distance	13.5km
Total ascent/descent	1300m
Grade	3
Time	5hr 30min
Refreshments	Refreshments at Refugi del Gresolet picnic site; none along the way.
Access	From the direction of Guardiola de Berguedà, leave the B-400 road on a track before the viaduct just outside Saldes towards Gresolet, which is about 6.5km away; this area is very popular with walkers so the quality of the dirt track is good.

This magnificent trail climbs Comabona (alt. 2548m) with some stunning views towards the nearby Pedraforca massif. You need to have your own transport to get to the starting point but your effort will be rewarded with tranquil, less trodden paths. Green/white signs mark most of the trail.

From Gresolet picnic site take the track downhill and then in the left-hand bend of the road go right. Cross the parking area and take the narrow path marked only with a red circle. Ascend steadily through forest. Reach a track, go left and a few minutes later leave it to the left on a path marked with a red circle.

Climb in a narrow gully through beech forest. Arrive on a track, go left and a few metres later in a roadbend take the path marked with a red circle. Continue to ascend, and when you reach the track again go left towards the signpost. At **Coll de Bauma** track junction keep left on the track; it is marked with green/white signs, as well as red/white (GR107) signs. A few minutes later at a junction go right towards 'Comabona (inici 9km)' through a **barrier**. (The path on the left is also marked with green/white signs, and you will return to this junction on that path.)

As you traverse this section, the rugged mountain of Pedraforca is behind you and forested mountains dominate the views on your right. Shortly after, leave this

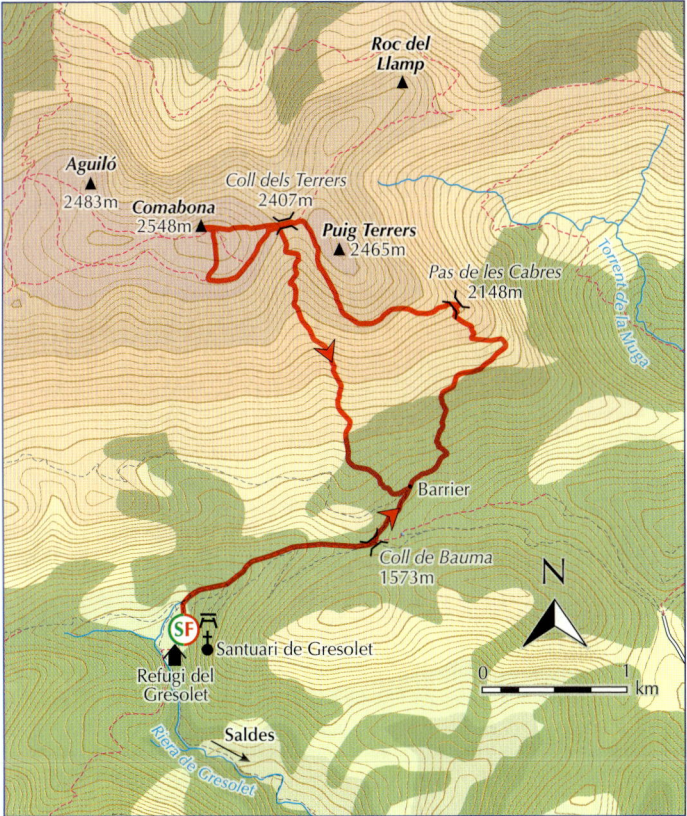

forest track to the left steeply uphill on a path towards Comabona. Follow the green/white signs on trees and rocks. Zigzag uphill through pine forest and then continue with more views of the Cadí-Moixeró mountain range. The trees peter out leaving the mountainside with only shrubs as the path curves left uphill.

Climb steeply on the grassy mountainside and then shortly after the path skirts below Puig Terrers. Pass a stone shelter and shortly Comabona comes into view. Soon you can spot the col where you make the final ascent to the top. Climb the often steep rocky path that heads towards Comabona and reach a granite waymarker at **Coll dels Terrers** (alt. 2407) about 2hr from Coll de Bauma.

145

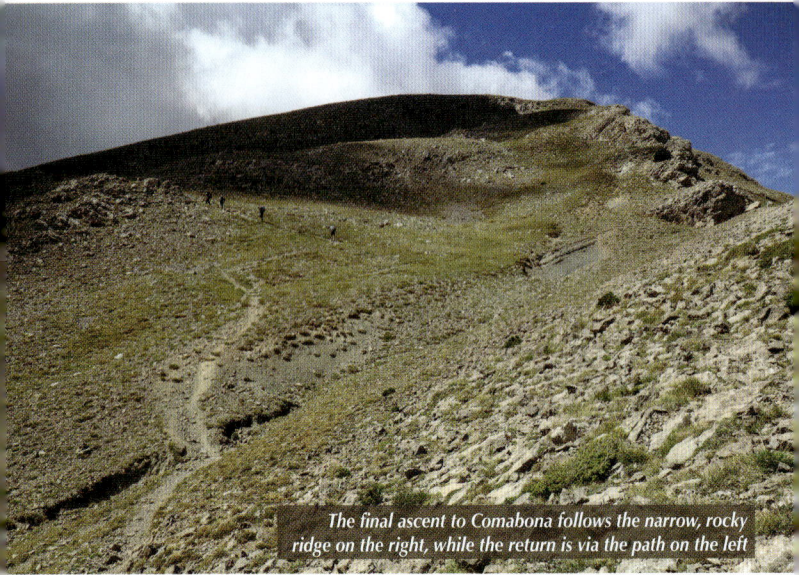

The final ascent to Comabona follows the narrow, rocky ridge on the right, while the return is via the path on the left

Keep slightly right and drop down to meet another path, and then keep left towards Comabona. As well as green/white there are red/white signs. Notice the path on the left, also marked with green/white signs, that heads down to the valley; you will take that path after visiting the summit. At first continue straight on uphill on the stony path. There are two paths; take the one closer to the edge on the right which climbs steeply to the summit of **Comabona** (alt. 2548m). From the peak enjoy the amazing panorama dominated by the nearby impressive Pedraforca massif. From the summit follow the green/white signs (sometimes hard to spot) south in the direction of Pedraforca, continuing downhill on the grassy slope until you meet a more prominent path; keep left and follow it back to the col. Alternatively retrace your steps from the summit back to Coll dels Terrers.

From the col take the path right downhill towards the valley, marked with green/white signs. Descend for nearly 1hr 30min, initially zigzagging downhill on the grassy hillside and then occasionally crossing scree fields. As you descend there are more and more trees. Walk through pine forest before you arrive back at the junction near the **barrier** (you took the path on the left towards Comabona). Go straight on the track back to **Coll de Bauma** and retrace your steps to **Gresolet picnic site** (about 30min).

WALK 35
Pedraforca 360

Start/finish	Plaça Major, Gósol, N42.237054, E1.660350
Distance	17.5km
Total ascent/descent	820m
Grade	2
Time	5hr 30min
Refreshments	Café, bar and bakery on Plaça Major in Gósol; Refugi Lluís Estasen.
Access	Gósol is located on the B-400 road, 9km east of Saldes – parking is available at the edge of the village.
Public transport	Buses from Berga and Bagà.

This signposted PR-C 127 route is also known as Pedraforca 360. As the name suggests, the route encircles the grand Pedraforca massif, allowing you to appreciate the magnificent views of Pedraforca on all sides without climbing the mighty mountain itself.

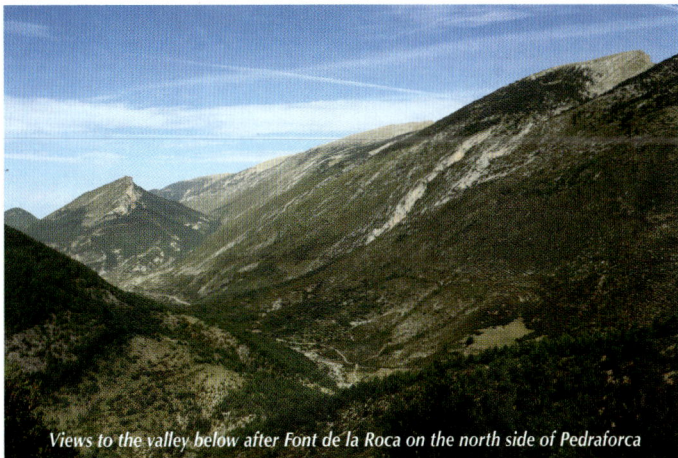

Views to the valley below after Font de la Roca on the north side of Pedraforca

Leave Plaça Major on the PR-C 123/PR-C 127 route on Carrer Picasso towards Font Terrers and El Collel. In 1906 Picasso spent a few months in Gósol staying at the inn. After the next signpost pass a wash house and a fountain with an ornate bull head on Plaça Augustí Pedro i Pons. Keep left and follow the yellow/white signs on Carrer Cerdanya. The road becomes a gravel track that you leave to the right uphill on a rocky path marked with yellow/white signs and red/white signs.

Ascend through forest and soon the path gets close to the road. At the junction with a signpost keep left towards Font Terrers (marked with GR107, PR-C 127 and PR-C 123 signs) with some views of the forested mountains to the west. Arrive on a track, go right and reach **Font Terrers** (alt. 1625m) and its picnic site. Walk across the parking area and keep right on the forest track. Follow it for 20 metres and then leave it on a path to the left passing the reservoir. The path is initially parallel to the track and marked with yellow/white and red/white signs. At Torrent de la Coma dels Caners path junction keep left towards El Collel and ascend through forest. As the trees peter out you have more views to the nearby mountains of the Cadí range.

Pass a spring, **Font de la Roca**, and spot a stone hut in the valley as you follow the path on the grassy mountainside. About 1hr 30min from Gósol reach a track by the signpost at **El Collell**. Keep right on the PR-C 127 route (the GR107 trail goes left) and follow the track downhill with the north side of Pedraforca dominating the views for nearly an hour.

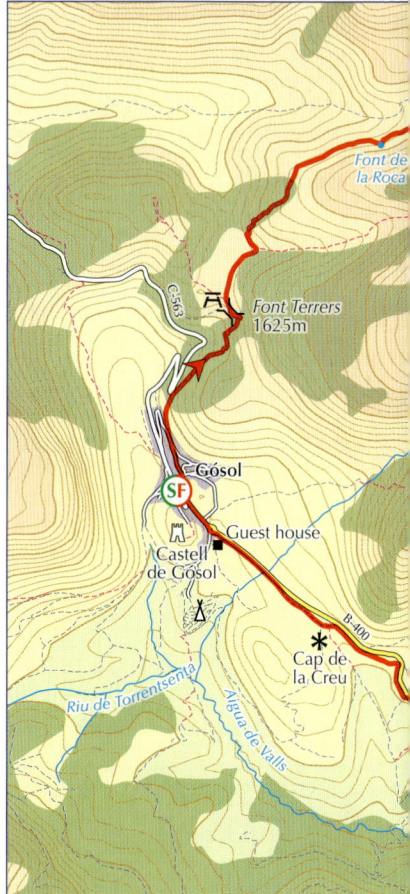

148

Leave the track to the right on a path with yellow/white signs uphill through forest, and a few minutes later reach **Refugi Lluís Estasen**. At the junction at the corner of the building continue on the PR-C 127 route towards Gósol.

Shortly after at the path junction with signpost keep left towards Gósol. Cross a scree and descend and at **La Serra (first junction)**; continue straight on and a few minutes later at **La Serra (second junction)** carry straight on towards Gósol

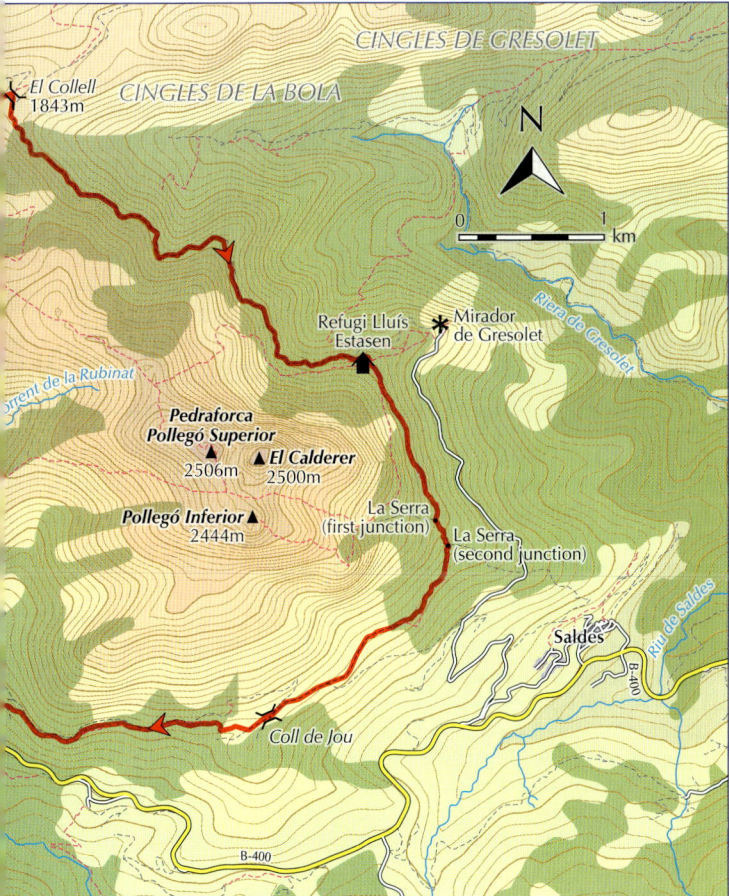

Refreshments are available at Refugi Lluís Estasen

per Coll de Jou. Pedraforca is towering on your right as you follow the yellow/white signs on the mountainside. The path becomes a rough track, and then at a clearing pass a boulder with a memorial plaque and the Pedraforca 360 symbol.

Meet another track and continue on the PR-C 127 straight on uphill. A few minutes later at **Coll de Jou**, at a track junction, go downhill towards a watering hole. After passing the watering hole (on your left) the track becomes a path. As you follow the undulating path through forest you can see the houses of l'Espa village on the left below. Shortly, the ruins of Castell de Gósol come into view. When the path widens follow the signs to the left, passing an abandoned house (on your left), and then descend to the road. Keep right on the footpath on the left-hand side of the road. Initially the path runs parallel to the road and then it slightly bends away. At **(Coll del) Cap de la Creu** continue straight on, follow the track parallel to the road and arrive back at **Gósol** by a guest house and restaurant at a roundabout, and continue straight on to the village centre.

APPENDIX A
Useful contacts and information

Tourist information

https://experience.catalunya.com

www.girona.cat

www.empordaturisme.com

www.turismegarrotxa.com

www.ripollesturisme.com

www.valldenuria.cat

www.visitpirineus.com

www.visitbergueda.com

www.vallter.cat

Tourist information centres

Garrotxa
Olot
Carrer Dr. Fàbregas, 6, 17800 Olot, Girona
www.turismeolot.cat
+34 972 260 141

La Vall d'en Bas
Passatge de Can Trona, 26, 17176 Joanetes, Girona
www.vallbas.cat
+34 972 692 177

Les Preses
Avinguda de l'Estació, 17178 Les Preses, Girona
www.lespreses.cat
+34 972 694 904

Besalú
Carrer del Pont, 1, 17850 Besalú Girona
www.besalu.cat
+34 972 591 240

Ripollès
Ripoll
Plaça de L'abat Oliba, s/n, 17500 Ripoll, Girona
www.visit.ripoll.cat
+34 972 702 351

Camprodon
Carrer Sant Roc, 22, 17867 Camprodon, Girona
www.valldecamprodon.org
+34 972 740 010

Ribes de Freser
Carretera Bruguera, 2, 17534 Ribes de Freser, Girona
www.vallderibes.cat
+34 972 727 728

Cadí-Moixeró Natural Park
Bagà
Carrer Pujada al Palau, 08695 Bagà, Barcelona
www.turismebaga.com
+34 619 746 099

Berguedà
Ctra. C-16, Km 96, 200, 08600 Berga, Barcelona
www.elbergueda.cat
+34 654 125 696

Travel

Air

www.girona-airport.net

www.barcelona-airport.com

www.britishairways.com

www.vueling.com

www.easyjet.com

www.ryanair.com

www.skyscanner.net

Train

www.renfe.com

www.valldenuria.cat – Vall de Núria rack railway

www.thetrainline.com

www.eurotunnel.com

Ferry

www.brittany-ferries.co.uk

www.directferries.co.uk

Bus

www.tmb.cat

www.teisa-bus.com

www.aquibergueda.cat/mobilitat/

www.aena.es

www.vallbas.cat/municipi/tad/
On demand bus in the Bas Valley

www.elbergueda.cat/en/planifica/com-arribar.htm

https://mobilitat.bergueda.cat

www.itinerannia.net/en/territory/how-to-get-there (train and bus)

Taxi

www.taxitourgarrotxa.com

Car rental

www.rentalcars.com

www.holidayautos.com

www.avis.com

www.autoeurope.com

www.centauro.net

www.goldcar.es

www.europecar.com

www.hertz.com

www.budget.com

www.sixt.com

APPENDIX B
Accommodation

www.gironacasesrurals.com

www.ripollesturisme.com

www.catalunya.com

www.travelsupermarket.com

www.trivago.com

www.airbnb.co.uk

www.booking.com

www.somrurals.com

Campsites

Garrotxa

Bassegoda Park
Camí de Bassegoda, s/n, 17733
Albanyà, Girona
www.bassegodapark.com
+34 972 542 020
info@bassegodapark.com

Càmping Montagut
Ctra. de Sadernes, km 2, 17855,
Montagut, Girona
www.campingmontagut.com
+34 661 673 057
info@campingmontagut.com

Càmping La Fageda
Ctra. Olot-Santa Pau, km 4, 17800 Olot,
Girona
www.campinglafageda.com
+34 972 271 239
info@campinglafageda.com

Ripollès

Càmping Els Roures
Av. El Mariner, 34–36, 17864 Sant Pau
de Segúries, Girona
www.elsroures.com
+34 972 747 000
reserves@elsroures.com

Càmping Vall de Camprodon
Ctra. C-38 Km 7.5 from Ripoll to
Camprodon 17867 Camprodon, Girona
www.valldecamprodon.net
+34 972 740 507info@
valldecamprodon.net

Càmping Conca de Ter
Ctra. Setcases s/n, 17869 Vilallonga de
Ter, Girona
www.concater.com
+34 972 740 629
concater@concater.com

Càmping Pirinenc
Ctra. Gombrèn, km 3, 17530
Campdevànol, Girona
www.campingpirinenc.com
+34 972 712 023
info@campingpirinenc.com

Càmping Vall de Ribes
Ctra. de Pardines, Km 0.5, 17534 Ribes
de Freser, Girona
www.campingvallderibes.com
+34 972 728 820
info@campinvallderibes.com

Cadí-Moixeró Natural Park

Càmping El Berguedà
Ctra. B-400 to Saldes km 3.5, 08694,
Barcelona
www.campingbergueda.com
+34 938 227 432

Càmping Repòs del Pedraforca
Ctra. B-400, km 13.5, 08697 Saldes,
Barcelona
www.campingpedraforca.com
+34 938 258 044
pedra@campingpedraforca.com

Càmping Bastareny
Carretera Gisclareny, km 1, 08695
Bagà, Barcelona
www.campingbastareny.com
+34 938 244 420
campingbastareny@gmail.com

APPENDIX C
Glossary

Catalan	Spanish	English
abelles	*abejas*	bees
aigua	*agua*	water
ajuntament	*ayuntamiento*	town hall
ambulància	*ambulancia*	ambulance
àrea d'esplai	*área de recreo*	recreation area
autobús	*autobús*	bus
autocaravana	*caravana*	campervan
avenc	*sima*	chasm
balma	*balma*	natural rock shelter
bebent aigua	*agua potable*	drinking water
bitllet	*billete*	ticket
bombers	*bomberos*	fire brigade
bon dia	*buenos días*	good morning
bona tarda	*buenos tardes*	good afternoon
bosc	*bosque*	forest
càmping	*cámping*	campsite
capella	*capilla*	chapel
carrer	*calle*	street
carretera	*carretera*	road
casa	*casa*	house
castell	*castillo*	castle
cavall	*caballo*	horse
cervesa	*cerveza*	beer
cim	*cima*	summit
coll	*coll*	col

Catalan	Spanish	English
cotxe	coche	car
cova	cueva	cave
dinar	almuerzo	lunch
elevació	elevación	elevation
emergència	emergencia	emergency
entrada	entrada	entrance
escola	escuela	school
església	iglesia	church
esmorzar	desayuno	breakfast
estació d'autobusos	estación de autobúses	bus station
estació de trene	stación de tren	railway station
excursionista	excursionista	hiker
foc	fuego	fire
font	fuente	spring
gorg, barranc	barranco	ravine
gosso	perro	dog
habitació	habitación	room
hola	hola	hello
horaris	horarios	timetable
mapa	mapa	map
masia	granja	farmhouse
mercat	mercado	market
mina	mina	mine
monastir	monasterio	monastery
muntanya	montaña	mountain
obert	abierto	open
oficina de turisme	oficina de turismo	tourist office

Catalan	Spanish	English
pantà, embassament	embalse	reservoir
parada d'autobús	parada de autobús	bus stop
parc natural	parque natural	natural park
perill	peligro	danger
policia	policía	police
pont	puente	bridge
presare	presa	dam
privat	privado	private
puig	pico	peak
refugire	fugio	refuge
riu, riera	río	river
roca	roca	rock
ruta, recorregud	ruta, recorrido	route
salt, cascada	cascada	waterfall
sendero, camí	sendero, camino	trail, path
sopar	cena	dinner
sortida	salida	exit
supermercat	supermercado	supermarket
tancat	cerrado	closed
tenda	tienda	tent
torrent, sot	torrente	stream
tren	tren	train
turisme rural	turismo rural	rural tourism
turó	cerro	hill
vaca	vaca	cow
vall	valle	valley
vi	vino	wine

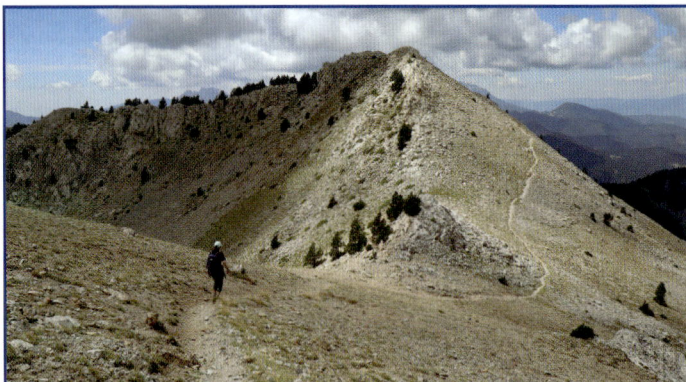

DOWNLOAD THE ROUTES
IN GPX FORMAT

All the routes in this guide are available for download from:

www.cicerone.co.uk/1163/GPX

as standard format GPX files. You should be able to load them into most online GPX systems and mobile devices, whether GPS or smartphone. You may need to convert the file into your preferred format using a conversion programme such as gpsvisualizer.com or one of the many other such websites and programmes.

When you follow this link, you will be asked for your email address and where you purchased the guidebook, and have the option to subscribe to the Cicerone e-newsletter.

CICERONE
www.cicerone.co.uk

LISTING OF CICERONE GUIDES

ALPS CROSS-BORDER ROUTES

100 Hut Walks in the Alps
Alpine Ski Mountaineering
  Vol 1 – Western Alps
The Karnischer Hohenweg
The Tour of the Bernina
Trail Running – Chamonix and the
  Mont Blanc region
Trekking Chamonix to Zermatt
Trekking in the Alps
Trekking in the Silvretta and
  Ratikon Alps
Trekking Munich to Venice
Trekking the Tour of Mont Blanc
Walking in the Alps

PYRENEES AND FRANCE/SPAIN
CROSS-BORDER ROUTES

Shorter Treks in the Pyrenees
The GR11 Trail
The Pyrenean Haute Route
The Pyrenees
Walks and Climbs in the Pyrenees

AUSTRIA

Innsbruck Mountain Adventures
Trekking Austria's Adlerweg
Trekking in Austria's Hohe Tauern
Trekking in Austria's Zillertal Alps
Trekking in the Stubai Alps
Walking in Austria
Walking in the Salzkammergut:
  the Austrian Lake District

FRANCE, BELGIUM
AND LUXEMBOURG

Camino de Santiago – Via Podiensis
Chamonix Mountain Adventures
Cycle Touring in France
Cycling London to Paris
Cycling the Canal de la Garonne
Cycling the Canal du Midi
Cycling the Route des Grandes Alpes
Mont Blanc Walks
Mountain Adventures in the
  Maurienne
Short Treks on Corsica
The GR5 Trail
The GR5 Trail – Benelux
  and Lorraine
The GR5 Trail – Vosges and Jura
The Grand Traverse of the
  Massif Central
The Moselle Cycle Route
The River Loire Cycle Route
The River Rhone Cycle Route
Trekking in the Vanoise
Trekking the Cathar Way

Trekking the GR10
Trekking the GR20 Corsica
Trekking the Robert Louis
  Stevenson Trail
Via Ferratas of the French Alps
Walking in Provence – East
Walking in Provence – West
Walking in the Ardennes
Walking in the Auvergne
Walking in the Briançonnais
Walking in the Dordogne
Walking in the Haute Savoie: North
Walking in the Haute Savoie: South
Walking on Corsica
Walking the Brittany Coast Path

GERMANY

Hiking and Cycling in the
  Black Forest
The Danube Cycleway Vol 1
The Rhine Cycle Route
The Westweg
Walking in the Bavarian Alps

ITALY

Alta Via 1 – Trekking in
  the Dolomites
Alta Via 2 – Trekking in
  the Dolomites
Day Walks in the Dolomites
Italy's Grande Traversata delle Alpi
Italy's Sibillini National Park
Ski Touring and Snowshoeing in
  the Dolomites
The Way of St Francis
Trekking in the Apennines
Trekking the Giants' Trail: Alta Via 1
  through the Italian Pennine Alps
Via Ferratas of the Italian Dolomites
  Vols 1&2
Walking and Trekking in the
  Gran Paradiso
Walking in Abruzzo
Walking in Italy's Cinque Terre
Walking in Italy's Stelvio
  National Park
Walking in Sicily
Walking in the Aosta Valley
Walking in the Dolomites
Walking in Tuscany
Walking in Umbria
Walking Lake Como and Maggiore
Walking Lake Garda and Iseo
Walking on the Amalfi Coast
Walking the Via Francigena
  Pilgrim Route – Parts 2&3
Walks and Treks in the
  Maritime Alps

MEDITERRANEAN

The High Mountains of Crete
Trekking in Greece
Walking and Trekking in Zagori
Walking and Trekking on Corfu
Walking in Cyprus
Walking on Malta
Walking on the Greek Islands –
  the Cyclades

SPAIN AND PORTUGAL

Camino de Santiago:
  Camino Frances
Coastal Walks in Andalucia
Costa Blanca Mountain Adventures
Cycling the Camino de Santiago
Cycling the Ruta Via de la Plata
Mountain Walking in Mallorca
Mountain Walking in
  Southern Catalunya
Portugal's Rota Vicentina
Spain's Sendero Historico: The GR1
The Andalucian Coast to Coast Walk
The Camino del Norte and
  Camino Primitivo
The Camino Ingles and Ruta do Mar
The Camino Portugues
The Mountains of Nerja
The Mountains of Ronda
  and Grazalema
The Sierras of Extremadura
Trekking in Mallorca
Trekking in the Canary Islands
Trekking the GR7 in Andalucia
Walking and Trekking in the
  Sierra Nevada
Walking in Andalucia
Walking in Catalunya – Barcelona
Walking in Catalunya – Girona
  Pyrenees
Walking in Portugal
Walking in the Algarve
Walking in the Picos de Europa
Walking on Gran Canaria
Walking on La Gomera and El Hierro
Walking on La Palma
Walking on Lanzarote
  and Fuerteventura
Walking on Madeira
Walking on Tenerife
Walking on the Azores
Walking on the Costa Blanca
Walking the Camino dos Faros

For full information on all our
guides, books and eBooks,
visit our website:
www.cicerone.co.uk

CICERONE

Trust Cicerone to guide your next adventure, wherever it may be around the world...

Discover guides for hiking, mountain walking, backpacking, trekking, trail running, cycling and mountain biking, ski touring, climbing and scrambling in Britain, Europe and worldwide.

Connect with Cicerone online and find inspiration.

- buy books and ebooks
- articles, advice and trip reports
- podcasts and live events
- GPX files and updates
- regular newsletter

cicerone.co.uk